Table of Contents

Introduction (Page 4)
- Why AI Voice Solutions? (Page 4)
- What This Book Will Cover (Page 5)
- What You'll Learn (Page 6)
- Who This Book Is For (Page 6)
- How to Use This Book (Page 7)

Chapter 1: Understanding AI Voice Solutions (Page 8)
- What Are AI Voice Solutions? (Page 8)
- Why They're Crucial for Small Businesses (Page 9)
- How They Work: A Simplified Explanation of NLP and ML (Page 10)
- Real-Life Scenarios: How Businesses Are Using AI Voice Solutions (Page 11)

Chapter 2: Essential Tools for AI Voice Assistants (Page 13)
- Overview of What's Needed (Page 13)
- Why You Need These Tools (Page 14)
- Step-by-Step Guide to Setting Up Each Tool (Page 15)
- Bringing It All Together (Page 23)

Chapter 3: Setting Up ChatGPT for Voice Prompts (Page 24)
- What Is ChatGPT, and Why Do We Use It? (Page 24)
- What Are Voice Prompts? (Page 24)
- Step-by-Step Guide to Using ChatGPT for Voice Prompts (Page 25)
- Extra Tips for Using ChatGPT (Page 30)

Chapter 4: Building Your AI Voice Assistant with Vapi.ai (**Page 32**)
- What Is Vapi.ai and Why Do We Use It? (Page 32)
- What You'll Need Before Starting (Page 33)
- Step-by-Step Guide to Setting Up Your AI Voice Assistant (Page 33)

Chapter 5: Automating Workflows with Make.com (**Page 41**)
- What Is Make.com and Why Do We Use It? (Page 41)
- What You'll Need Before Starting (Page 42)
- Step-by-Step Guide to Setting Up Automation with make.com (Page 43)

Chapter 6: Adding Telephony Features with Twilio (**Page 50**)
- What Is Twilio and Why Do We Use It? (Page 50)
- What You'll Need Before Starting (Page 51)
- Step-by-Step Guide to Setting Up Twilio (Page 51)

Chapter 7: Putting It All Together – Integrating and Optimizing Your AI Voice Solution (**Page 59**)
- What Does "Putting It All Together" Mean? (Page 59)
- What You'll Need Before We Start (Page 60)
- Step-by-Step Guide to Integrating Everything (Page 60)

Chapter 8: Real-World Use Cases and Best Practices (**Page 67**)
- Use Case 1: AI Receptionist for a Medical Clinic (Page 68)
- Use Case 2: AI Customer Service Agent for an E-commerce Store (Page 83)
- Use Case 3: AI Cold Caller for a Real Estate Agency (Page 92)
- Use Case 4: AI Customer Retention Specialist for a Subscription-Based Business (Page 100)

Chapter 9: Data Security and Compliance (Page 108)

- Why Data Security and Ethical AI Matter (Page 108)
- Part 1: Protecting Customer Data (Page 108)
- Part 2: Ensuring Ethical AI Use (Page 112)

Chapter 10: Future Trends in AI Voice Solutions (Page 115)

- Preparing for the Future of AI (Page 115)
- Emerging Trends in AI Voice Solutions (Page 115)
- Preparing for the Future (Page 120)

Conclusion (Page 123)

What's Next? A Series to Help You Master AI (Page 128)

Glossary of Terms (Page 130)

Appendices (Page 133)

Introduction

Welcome to AI Voice Solutions for Small Businesses - A Practical Guide!

Imagine this: A small dental clinic, overwhelmed by the daily grind of managing appointment calls and answering repetitive inquiries. Patients were frustrated with long wait times, and staff felt stretched thin. But everything changed when they introduced an AI voice assistant. With over **40 hours per month** saved on administrative tasks and a **25% reduction in missed appointments**, the clinic experienced smoother operations, happier patients, and a more focused team.

Now picture a real estate agency struggling to keep up with cold calls and lead generation. By automating these tasks with an AI-powered assistant, they saw a **30% boost in client engagement** within three months—all while their agents focused on closing deals and building relationships.

These are just two examples of how AI voice solutions are transforming small businesses. In fact, studies show that **70% of small businesses** plan to adopt AI technologies by 2025, with voice automation at the forefront of this revolution. Whether it's streamlining operations, improving customer service, or creating scalable systems, AI is levelling the playing field, empowering businesses like yours to compete and thrive.

Why AI Voice Solutions?

In today's fast-paced, customer-driven world, expectations are high. Clients want seamless, personalized, and immediate service, while small businesses face the challenge of delivering excellence with limited resources. Tight budgets, long hours, and competing priorities can make it feel impossible to keep up.

AI voice solutions offer a way forward. Imagine having a reliable assistant who works 24/7, handles hundreds of customer interactions simultaneously, and never gets tired. From answering inquiries and scheduling appointments to generating leads and following up with clients, AI voice assistants free you and your team to focus on what you do best—growing your business and delighting your customers.

And the best part? This isn't technology reserved for large corporations. With the right tools, AI voice solutions are accessible, affordable, and adaptable for businesses of all sizes.

What This Book Will Cover

This guide is your step-by-step roadmap to integrating AI voice solutions into your business. We'll explore four powerful tools that make this transformation simple and effective:

- **ChatGPT**: Create natural, engaging conversational scripts for your AI assistant.

- **Vapi.ai**: Build and customize an AI-powered voice assistant to handle calls and automate tasks.

- **Make.com**: Connect your AI assistant to your CRM, calendar, and other business tools for seamless workflows.

- **Twilio**: Power your communication channels with professional-grade phone and SMS capabilities.

Together, these tools form a complete, user-friendly solution to help you modernize your business operations.

What You'll Learn

This book is designed to be actionable, even if you're not a tech expert. Here's what you'll gain:

- **AI Voice Technology Basics**: Understand how AI works and why it's perfect for small businesses.
- **Step-by-Step Tool Setup**: Follow clear instructions to set up and connect ChatGPT, Vapi.ai, Make.com, and Twilio.
- **Workflow Automation**: Learn how to streamline repetitive tasks and save time.
- **Real-World Case Studies**: Discover how small businesses in industries like healthcare, retail, and real estate have successfully adopted AI.
- **Best Practices**: Get expert tips on writing effective scripts, optimizing processes, and ensuring a great customer experience.

Who This Book Is For

Whether you're a solopreneur, a small business owner, or a manager, this guide is for anyone who wants to embrace cutting-edge technology without needing an IT team or technical expertise.

From dental clinics and law firms to e-commerce stores and real estate agencies, the tools and strategies in this book are adaptable to your unique needs and goals.

Why These Tools?

We've chosen ChatGPT, Vapi.ai, Make.com, and Twilio for their simplicity, effectiveness, and seamless integration. Together, they create a robust solution that's easy to implement and highly impactful:

- **ChatGPT**: Ensures natural, engaging conversations that reflect your brand's tone.
- **Vapi.ai**: Powers intelligent voice recognition and responsive call handling.
- **Make.com**: Automates workflows, reducing manual work and saving time.
- **Twilio**: Adds professional-grade phone and SMS capabilities for seamless communication.

This combination makes AI voice solutions accessible and scalable for businesses of any size.

How to Use This Book

You don't need to read this book cover to cover—feel free to jump to the sections most relevant to your needs. If you're new to AI voice solutions, we recommend starting from the beginning. Each chapter builds on the last, guiding you from understanding the basics to launching your AI system and automating your business processes.

By the time you finish, you'll have a fully functioning AI voice assistant customized to your business. More importantly, you'll gain the knowledge and confidence to leverage this technology for long-term success.

The future of communication is here. It's time to embrace it. Let's get started!

Chapter 1: Understanding AI Voice Solutions

What Are AI Voice Solutions?

AI Voice Solutions are advanced systems powered by Artificial Intelligence (AI) that can understand, interpret, and respond to human speech. These solutions use cutting-edge technologies such as Natural Language Processing (NLP) and Machine Learning (ML) to enable machines to communicate in ways that sound and feel natural.

AI Voice Assistants are the backbone of these solutions. They can perform a wide variety of tasks, including answering phone calls, scheduling appointments, managing customer inquiries, and even making sales calls. Unlike traditional automated systems that rely on rigid scripts and pre-recorded messages, AI voice assistants can have dynamic, conversational interactions, adapting to the needs of the person on the other end of the line.

Let's take a look at the two core technologies that make these solutions possible:

- **Natural Language Processing (NLP)**: This is the technology that allows AI to understand and interpret human language. It breaks down spoken words into data, analyzes their meaning, and formulates a suitable response.
- **Machine Learning (ML)**: This enables the AI to learn from interactions and improve over time. The more conversations the AI has, the smarter and more accurate it becomes at understanding and responding to different types of questions and requests.

Why They're Crucial for Small Businesses

Small businesses operate with limited resources and often struggle to balance the need for excellent customer service with the realities of their budgets and staff availability. AI voice solutions are crucial because they offer several game-changing benefits:

1. **Cost Savings**: Hiring and training staff for routine tasks, like answering phones or booking appointments, can be expensive. AI voice assistants handle these tasks automatically, reducing the need for a large administrative team and saving money in the long run.
2. **24/7 Availability**: Your business might be closed after hours, but that doesn't mean your customers stop needing assistance. AI voice assistants can work around the clock, answering calls, providing information, and booking appointments even when you're off the clock.
3. **Enhanced Customer Experience**: With AI voice solutions, customers get immediate, consistent, and accurate responses. There are no long wait times, no miscommunication, and no dropped calls. This leads to a higher level of customer satisfaction and increased loyalty.
4. **Scalability**: As your business grows, so does the demand for efficient customer service. AI voice assistants can easily scale to handle higher call volumes without needing additional human resources.
5. **Consistency**: AI assistants deliver consistent performance, free from human errors or variations in service quality. Every customer gets the same high standard of service.

In short, AI voice solutions provide small businesses with the ability to offer top-notch customer service while saving on costs and improving operational efficiency.

How They Work: A Simplified Explanation of NLP and ML

To make AI voice assistants work effectively, two primary technologies come into play:

1. **Natural Language Processing (NLP):**

   - **Understanding Speech**: When a customer speaks to the AI, NLP technology converts the spoken words into a format the AI can understand. It identifies key phrases, detects the intention behind the words, and extracts relevant information.
   - **Generating Responses**: Once the AI understands the customer's request, NLP helps the assistant generate a clear and appropriate response. This is what allows AI assistants to have fluid, human-like conversations, rather than sounding robotic or scripted.
   - **Handling Accents and Variations**: NLP systems are trained to understand different accents, speech patterns, and colloquialisms. This means that no matter how your customers speak, the AI can still provide accurate and relevant answers.

2. **Machine Learning (ML):**

   - **Learning and Adapting**: Machine Learning allows the AI to improve over time. By analyzing past interactions, the AI gets better at predicting what a customer might need and refining its responses.
   - **Adapting to New Information**: If your business introduces a new service or product, the AI can be trained to understand and explain it. ML ensures the assistant stays up-to-date with changes, continually improving its usefulness and accuracy

Together, NLP and ML create a system that not only listens to what your customers are saying but also understands and responds in a way that feels natural and helpful.

Real-Life Scenarios: How Businesses Are Using AI Voice Solutions

Let's explore some practical examples of how businesses are leveraging AI voice solutions to streamline operations and improve customer service:

1. **Example 1: AI Receptionist for a Medical Clinic**

   - **Challenge**: The clinic was overwhelmed with phone calls from patients trying to schedule appointments or ask about services, causing delays and patient frustration.
   - **Solution**: An AI receptionist was set up to handle these calls. It could book appointments, provide information on clinic hours and services, and forward emergency calls to a human staff member.
   - **Results**: The clinic saw a significant reduction in hold times, and patients appreciated the immediate, 24/7 service.

2. **Example 2: AI Customer Service for an E-commerce Store**

   - **Challenge**: Customers frequently called to check on order statuses, ask about return policies, or get product information. The store's limited staff couldn't keep up with the demand.
   - **Solution**: An AI customer service agent was implemented to answer common questions, process returns, and provide updates on orders.
   - **Results**: The store experienced fewer missed calls, higher customer satisfaction, and a more efficient use of their human staff, who could now focus on complex customer inquiries.

Example 3: AI Cold Caller for a Real Estate Agency

- **Challenge**: The agency needed to generate more leads but didn't have the resources to hire additional sales staff.
- **Solution**: An AI cold caller was programmed to make outbound calls, qualify leads, and schedule appointments for the human agents.
- **Results**: The AI cold caller successfully generated and pre-qualified leads, freeing up the real estate agents to focus on closing deals rather than making cold calls.

Example 4: AI Voice Assistant for a Law Firm

- **Challenge**: The firm received a high volume of calls from clients seeking updates on their cases, billing information, or general inquiries.
- **Solution**: An AI voice assistant was set up to handle routine inquiries and route more complex issues to the appropriate lawyer.
- **Results**: The firm saved hours of administrative work each week and clients were happier with the prompt service.

Key Takeaway

AI voice solutions aren't just for tech giants; they're incredibly valuable for small businesses, too. They offer an efficient, scalable way to improve customer service, cut down on operational costs, and free up your staff for more meaningful work. In the next chapter, we'll dive into the specific tools you'll need—ChatGPT, Vapi.ai, Make.com, and Twilio—and how to set them up to start reaping these benefits. Let's continue on this journey to modernize and simplify your business operations with AI!

Chapter 2: Essential Tools for AI Voice Assistants

Implementing AI Voice Solutions may seem daunting at first, but don't worry. This chapter will walk you through each tool you'll need, explain why it's essential, and show you how to set everything up in simple terms. By the end of this chapter, you'll be equipped to start building and customizing your AI voice assistant.

Overview of What's Needed

To get your AI voice assistant up and running, you'll need four main tools:

1. **ChatGPT**: A powerful language model developed by OpenAI to help you create natural, engaging, and conversational scripts for your AI assistant.
    - **Link**: OpenAI - ChatGPT

2. **Vapi.ai**: A platform that powers your AI assistant, enabling it to handle calls, understand customer requests, and respond intelligently.
    - **Link**: Vapi.ai

3. **Make.com**: An automation tool (formerly Integromat) that connects your AI assistant to other systems like Google Calendar, your email, or CRM software. It automates workflows, saving you time and effort.
    - **Link**: Make.com

4. **Twilio**: A communication platform that handles phone calls and SMS messages, allowing your AI assistant to interact with your customers via phone.
    - **Link**: Twilio

Why You Need These Tools

- **ChatGPT**: AI voice assistants are only as good as the words they say. ChatGPT helps you craft scripts that make your AI sound natural, professional, and engaging. You'll use it to create everything from greetings to responses for common questions.

- **Vapi.ai**: This tool serves as the brain of your AI assistant. It manages the conversations, uses NLP to understand speech, and responds in a way that feels human-like.

- **Make.com**: It simplifies automation by connecting your AI assistant to the tools you already use. For example, when your AI assistant books an appointment, Make.com can automatically add it to your calendar and send a confirmation email to your client.

- **Twilio**: Essential for handling phone-based interactions. Twilio enables your AI to make and receive calls and send text messages, making your communication seamless and professional.

Step-by-Step Guide to Setting Up Each Tool

Let's break down how to set up each tool in a way that's easy to follow, even if you're not tech-savvy.

Step 1: Setting Up ChatGPT

Why ChatGPT? ChatGPT is used to generate the voice prompts and responses for your AI assistant. It helps your assistant sound human and adapt to different scenarios.

How to Set Up ChatGPT:

1. **Sign Up for ChatGPT**: Go to [OpenAI - ChatGPT](https://openai.com/chatgpt) and create an account. You may have to select a plan, so consider starting with the free version if available to get a feel for the tool.

2. **Generating Voice Prompts**:
   - **Example**: Type in a prompt like, "Create a friendly greeting for a receptionist AI that answers customer calls."
   - **Result**: ChatGPT will generate a script like, "Hello! You've reached [Your Business Name]. How can I assist you today?"

3. **Customizing Scripts**: Modify the output to better fit your business needs. If you run a medical clinic, for example, you could adjust the greeting to, "Hello! You've reached [Clinic Name]. Are you calling to book an appointment or speak to a nurse?"

4. **Save Your Scripts**: Organize and save these scripts because you'll need to upload them to Vapi.ai.

Tips for Effective Prompts:

- **Be Specific**: When asking ChatGPT to create a script, provide as much detail as possible. Instead of saying, "Write a response," say, "Write a polite response for when a customer asks about our return policy."

- **Test Different Scenarios**: Create multiple variations of scripts for different customer situations. This way, your AI can respond appropriately no matter what the customer asks

Step 2: Setting Up Vapi.ai

Vapi.ai serves as the backbone of your AI assistant. It uses advanced Natural Language Processing (NLP) to understand customer conversations and provide tailored responses. Whether it's answering calls, booking appointments, or handling customer inquiries, Vapi.ai ensures smooth and professional interactions.

Why Vapi.ai?

Think of Vapi.ai as the engine that powers your AI assistant. While other tools like ChatGPT help craft conversational scripts, Vapi.ai transforms those scripts into actionable conversations. It enables your assistant to understand human speech, respond appropriately, and even handle call management.

Let's walk through how to set up Vapi.ai step by step:

1. Sign Up for Vapi.ai

- Open your web browser and navigate to Vapi.ai.
- Click on **"Sign Up"** at the top right of the homepage.
- Enter your email address and create a secure password.
- Check your inbox for a confirmation email and follow the instructions to verify your account.

Tip: Use an email you check often, as Vapi.ai will send updates and alerts about your assistant's performance.

2. Create a New Assistant

- Access the Vapi.ai Dashboard after logging in.
- Click on **"Create New Assistant"** to start.
- Choose a descriptive name for your assistant, such as *"AI Receptionist"* or *"Customer Support Bot."*
- Select the tone and voice of your assistant. Vapi.ai offers a variety of options, from formal and professional to warm and friendly.

3. Configure Call Handling

- **Greeting Scenarios**: Draft a friendly introduction like, "Thank you for calling [Your Business Name]. How can I assist you today?"

- **FAQ Responses**: Add responses for common questions like:
    - "What are your business hours?"
    - "Where are you located?"

- **Fallbacks**: Prepare for scenarios where the assistant doesn't understand the query. For example:
    - "I'm sorry, I don't have that information. Let me connect you to a team member."

- Set up call routing rules:
    - Route specific queries, like appointment-related questions, to the scheduling module.
    - Forward unanswered queries to a human representative.

4. Upload or Write Your Scripts

- **Open the "Scripts" Tab**: Navigate to the assistant's settings and locate the **"Scripts"** section.

- **Upload Pre-Written Scripts**: If you've already crafted scripts, such as those generated using ChatGPT, you can upload them directly. ChatGPT is an excellent tool for creating polished, conversational scripts tailored to your business needs.

- **Write New Scripts**: Use Vapi.ai built-in editor to create scripts for common scenarios, like:
    - Greeting Customers
    - Booking Appointments
    - Handling Complaints

- **Assign Actions or Triggers**: Link each script to specific actions or triggers, such as keywords or customer questions, to ensure smooth and relevant responses.

5. Test Your AI Assistant

Testing is a critical step to ensure your AI assistant delivers smooth and professional interactions. This process allows you to evaluate how well your assistant responds to customer queries, handles different scenarios, and transitions between tasks.

Run Test Calls

- Use the **Testing Tools** in the Vapi.ai dashboard to simulate various customer interactions.
- Try different scenarios, including:
    - Standard inquiries (e.g., "What are your hours?" or "Can I book an appointment?").
    - Edge cases (e.g., unusual questions or incomplete sentences).

        - Complex transitions (e.g., moving from a general inquiry to an appointment booking).
- Test for both voice and text responses if your assistant supports multiple interaction modes.

Observe Performance

- Pay close attention to how the assistant responds:
    - Is the tone appropriate for your brand?
    - Are the answers accurate and aligned with the scripts?
    - Does it handle transitions smoothly between scenarios?
    - Are fallback responses triggered appropriately for unrecognized inputs?

Common Issues to Look For

- **Misunderstandings**: Check if the assistant misinterprets certain phrases or accents.
- **Tone and Flow**: Ensure the tone matches your brand personality and flows naturally.
- **Gaps in Coverage**: Identify scenarios where the assistant might lack an appropriate response or fail to escalate to a human representative.

Refine and Improve

- Use insights from the test calls to make adjustments:
    - **Scripts**: Rewrite or expand scripts for scenarios where responses were unclear or inadequate.
    - **Call Flow**: Modify how the assistant navigates between tasks, ensuring smoother transitions.
    - **Tone**: Adjust the voice settings if the tone feels too formal, casual, or robotic for your audience.

- Test repeatedly until the assistant delivers consistent and satisfactory performance.

Simulate Real-World Conditions

- Conduct tests that mimic actual customer interactions, such as:
  - Background noise to assess how well the assistant understands speech in less-than-ideal conditions.
  - Varying speech speeds and accents to test the assistant's comprehension.
  - Overlapping inputs (e.g., interruptions) to see how it handles disruptions.

Gather Feedback

- If possible, involve colleagues or a small group of customers in testing. Their feedback can provide valuable insights into the assistant's usability and effectiveness.

Monitor Key Metrics

- Check metrics provided by Vapi.ai's analytics during testing, such as:
  - Response time
  - Completion rate for tasks like appointment booking
  - Frequency of fallback triggers or escalations

Testing ensures your AI assistant performs reliably, accurately, and in line with your business objectives. A well-tested assistant not only improves customer satisfaction but also reduces the need for human intervention, saving time and resources.

Step 3: Automating Workflows with make.com

Why Make.com? Make.com connects your AI assistant to your other business tools. It automates repetitive tasks, ensuring a seamless flow of information between systems.

How to Set Up Make.com:

1. **Sign Up on Make.com**: Visit Make.com and create an account. The platform is user-friendly, with templates and guides to help you set up.

2. **Create a New Scenario**:
   - Click "Create New Scenario" and choose Vapi.ai as your starting point.
   - Define what should happen when a specific event occurs, like, "When a new appointment is booked."

3. **Connect Your Tools**:
   - Example: If the AI books an appointment, Make.com can add it to Google Calendar, send a confirmation email to the client, and update your CRM.
   - You can also create workflows for things like logging customer inquiries or sending follow-up messages.

4. **Testing Your Workflow**: Run the scenario to ensure everything works smoothly. If there are any issues, adjust the settings until you're satisfied.

Common Automation Examples:

- **Appointment Reminders**: Automatically send a reminder email or SMS to clients 24 hours before their appointment.
- **Data Logging**: Store call details (like caller name and phone number) in a Google Sheet for future reference.

Step 4: Setting Up Twilio for Phone Communication

Why Twilio? Twilio is essential for enabling your AI assistant to make and receive phone calls. It also handles SMS communication, making it perfect for sending reminders or updates.

How to Set Up Twilio:

1. **Sign Up for Twilio**: Go to Twilio and create an account. Twilio offers a free trial with limited credits to help you get started.

2. **Get a Phone Number**:
   - In your Twilio dashboard, purchase a phone number. This will be the number your AI assistant uses to make and receive calls.

3. **Integrate with Vapi.ai**:
   - In Vapi.ai, go to the telephony settings and select Twilio as your provider.
   - Enter your Twilio API credentials (you can find these in your Twilio account settings).

4. **Configure Call Settings**:
   - Set up rules for call forwarding, voicemail, and SMS notifications.
   - **Example**: If the AI can't assist a caller, you can have Twilio forward the call to a human agent or send a text message with further instructions.

Testing and Finalizing:

- Test your Twilio setup by making a few calls and ensuring your AI assistant responds correctly. Also, try sending and receiving SMS to verify that everything works as expected.

Bringing It All Together

By now, you should have a clear understanding of how to set up ChatGPT, Vapi.ai, Make.com, and Twilio to build a robust AI voice assistant for your business. Here's a quick recap:

1. **ChatGPT**: Creates engaging and professional scripts for your AI assistant.
2. **Vapi.ai**: Powers the assistant, enabling it to handle calls and conversations.
3. **Make.com**: Automates your workflows, making your operations more efficient.
4. **Twilio**: Manages phone and SMS communication, adding a professional touch to your customer interactions.

Final Thoughts

Setting up an AI voice assistant may require a bit of time and experimentation, but once it's up and running, the benefits are immense. You'll have an automated system that can handle repetitive tasks, freeing up your staff to focus on more meaningful work. In the next chapter, we'll dive deeper into building specific types of AI voice assistants, like an AI receptionist or AI cold caller, and customizing them for your unique needs.

Let's move forward and continue building a more efficient, scalable, and customer-friendly business!

Chapter 3: Setting Up ChatGPT for Voice Prompts

Welcome to Chapter 3! This chapter will guide you through the process of using ChatGPT to create voice prompts for your AI voice assistant. Don't worry if you have no technical experience or prior knowledge. We'll keep things simple, detailed, and easy to understand. By the end of this chapter, you'll have a set of customized scripts ready to be used in your AI voice assistant.

What Is ChatGPT, and Why Do We Use It?

ChatGPT is an AI language model developed by OpenAI. It's designed to understand and generate human-like text. Think of it as a scriptwriting assistant that can create conversational

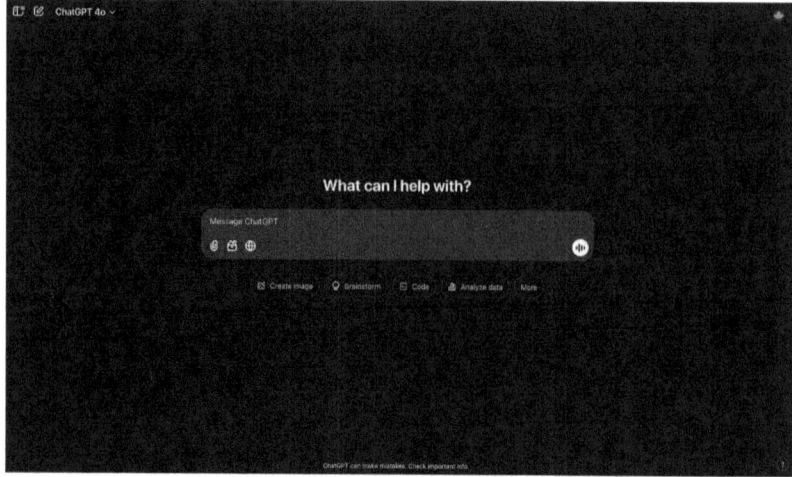

Instead of writing all the scripts yourself, you can give ChatGPT a few instructions, and it will generate natural and professional-sounding text that you can use to make your AI assistant sound engaging and helpful.

What Are Voice Prompts?

Voice prompts are the sentences or phrases your AI assistant will use to communicate with your customers. These include greetings, responses to common questions, instructions, and ways to handle unexpected queries. Well-written prompts are crucial for making your AI assistant feel friendly, approachable, and professional.

Step-by-Step Guide to Using ChatGPT for Voice Prompts

Let's get into the details, one step at a time.

Step 1: Signing Up for ChatGPT
Before we start creating scripts, you'll need to set up an account with OpenAI.

1. **Go to OpenAI's Website**: Visit [OpenAI - ChatGPT](#).

2. **Sign Up or Log In**:
    - If you're new to OpenAI, click on the "Sign Up" button and follow the instructions to create an account using your email address.
    - If you already have an account, just click "Log In" and enter your credentials.

1. **Choose a Plan**: OpenAI offers both free and paid plans. If you're trying this out for the first time, you can use the free plan. However, if you need more advanced features or frequent use, consider upgrading to a paid plan.

Step 2: Understanding Your Business Needs

Before you start generating scripts, it's essential to understand what your AI assistant will be doing for your business. Ask yourself:

1. **What types of interactions will my AI handle?**
   - Will it answer phone calls and greet customers?
   - Will it schedule appointments?
   - Will it answer common questions about your products or services?
   - Will it handle complaints or objections?

2. **What tone should my AI use?**
   - **Friendly and casual**: Great for a family restaurant or a local pet shop.
   - **Professional and formal**: Ideal for a law firm or medical clinic.
   - **Energetic and upbeat**: Suitable for a gym or fitness center.

3. **What common questions or requests do my customers have?**
   - Examples: "What are your business hours?" or "Can I book an appointment?"

Take a few minutes to jot down these needs. This preparation will make it easier to create scripts tailored to your business.

Step 3: Generating Voice Prompts with ChatGPT

Now that you understand your needs, let's create scripts using ChatGPT. Here's how to do it.

Example 1: Greeting and Introduction

The greeting is the first thing your customers will hear, so it should be warm and welcoming.

1. **Input Prompt for ChatGPT**: Type the following into ChatGPT:
   - "Write a friendly greeting for an AI receptionist at a dental clinic."

2. **ChatGPT Response**:
   - "Hello! You've reached [Your Dental Clinic Name]. I'm here to help you book an appointment, answer your questions, or connect you with the right person. How can I assist you today?"

Example 2: Appointment Scheduling

If your business requires appointment bookings, you'll need a script for that.

1. **Input Prompt for ChatGPT**:
   - "Create a script for an AI assistant booking an appointment at a spa."

2. **ChatGPT Response**:
   - "I'd be happy to help you schedule an appointment! Could you please let me know your preferred date and time? I'll check our availability and book you in right away."

Example 3: Answering FAQs

Think about the most common questions your customers ask. For example, questions about your business hours or return policy.

1. **Input Prompt for ChatGPT**:
   - "Write a response for when a customer asks about the return policy at a clothing store."
2. **ChatGPT Response**:
   - "Our return policy allows returns within 30 days of purchase, as long as the items are unworn and have the original tags attached. Would you like more details on how to make a return?"

Example 4: Handling Objections or Complaints

It's important to be prepared for situations where customers are upset or have concerns.

1. **Input Prompt for ChatGPT**:
   - "Create a polite response for when a customer is unhappy with a delayed delivery."
2. **ChatGPT Response**:
   - "I'm really sorry to hear about the delay with your delivery. Let me check the status for you and see what we can do to resolve this as quickly as possible. We truly appreciate your patience and understanding."

Example 5: Sales and Upselling

If your AI assistant is helping with sales, you'll want persuasive scripts.

1. **Input Prompt for ChatGPT**:
   - "Write a script for an AI cold caller encouraging a potential customer to schedule a property tour."

2. **ChatGPT Response**:
    - "Hi there! I'm calling from [Real Estate Agency Name]. We have some beautiful properties that match what you're looking for. Would you be interested in scheduling a tour to see them for yourself? I'd be happy to arrange that at your convenience."

Step 4: Customizing Your Voice Prompts

ChatGPT will generate responses that are pretty good, but you may need to tweak them to match your brand's voice perfectly. Here's how to do that:

1. **Adjust the Tone**: Make sure the language matches your desired tone. If the response is too formal, make it more relaxed. If it's too casual, make it more professional.
    - **Example**: Change "Hi there!" to "Good afternoon" if you want a more formal greeting.
2. **Add Specific Details**: Include the name of your business, specific product details, or anything else relevant.
    - **Example**: Instead of "our return policy," say, "At [Your Store Name], our return policy…"
3. **Ensure Clarity**: Make sure the scripts are easy to understand and sound natural when spoken.

Step 5: Organizing and Saving Your Scripts

Once you're happy with the scripts, it's important to save them in an organized way for easy access.

1. **Create a Folder on Your Computer**: Name it "AI Voice Assistant Scripts."

2. **Save Each Script as a Separate File**: Use clear and descriptive file names like "Greeting_Script," "Appointment_Booking," or "FAQ_Response."
3. **Use a Spreadsheet for Organization**: You can also create a spreadsheet to keep track of all your scripts and note which scenario each script is for.

Step 6: Testing and Refining Your Prompts

1. **Read Scripts Out Loud**: Speak each script out loud to see how it sounds. Does it flow naturally? Are there any awkward phrases?
2. **Get Feedback**: Ask colleagues, friends, or family members to listen to the scripts and give feedback. They might notice things you missed.
3. **Refine as Needed**: Use the feedback to make adjustments. For example, if a script sounds too robotic, simplify the language or add a friendly phrase.

Extra Tips for Using ChatGPT

- **Experiment with Different Prompts**: If you're not happy with the first response, try rephrasing your input. For example, instead of "Write a greeting," try "Create a welcoming greeting that feels friendly and warm."

- **Use Variations for Flexibility**: Create a few different versions of each script. This can make your AI assistant feel more dynamic and less repetitive.

- **Prepare for Unusual Questions**: Think about rare or unexpected scenarios and create scripts for them. This will make your AI assistant more versatile.

Example Summary of a Script Library

Here's what your script library might look like:

1. **Greeting_Script.txt**: "Hello! You've reached [Business Name]. How can I assist you today?"
2. **Appointment_Booking.txt**: "I'd be happy to book an appointment for you. What date and time work best?"
3. **FAQ_Response_BusinessHours.txt**: "Our business hours are Monday to Friday, 9 AM to 5 PM. How else can I help you?"
4. **Complaint_Response.txt**: "I apologize for the inconvenience. Let me look into this for you and find a solution."
5. **Sales_ColdCall.txt**: "Hi! I'm calling from [Company Name]. We have some great offers. Would you be interested in learning more?

Key Takeaways

- **ChatGPT Simplifies Script Creation**: Use it to generate natural-sounding responses that are easy to customize.

- **Be Organized**: Save your scripts in a well-organized folder for quick access.

- **Test and Adjust**: Make sure your scripts sound good and are easy for customers to understand.

Now that you have your scripts ready, it's time to move on to the next step: building your AI voice assistant using Vapi.ai. We'll cover that in the next chapter, so get ready to bring your AI assistant to life!

Chapter 4: Building Your AI Voice Assistant with Vapi.ai

Welcome to Chapter 4! In this chapter, we'll walk you through setting up your AI voice assistant using **Vapi.ai**. If you have no prior experience with AI or tech tools, don't worry. We'll cover everything step-by-step, with simple explanations to make the process easy to follow. By the end of this chapter, you'll have a fully functional AI assistant, ready to interact with your customers.

What Is Vapi.ai and Why Do We Use It?

Vapi.ai is a platform that allows you to build and customize AI voice assistants using Natural Language Processing (NLP). It's like the "brain" of your AI assistant, understanding what customers say and responding in a helpful, human-like way. Vapi.ai makes it simple to set up your assistant, even if you're not a tech expert.

Why Vapi.ai?

- **User-Friendly**: You don't need to write any code to get started.
- **Customizable**: You can upload your scripts and set specific behaviors to fit your business needs.
- **Powerful NLP**: Vapi.ai uses advanced technology to understand and interpret spoken language accurately.

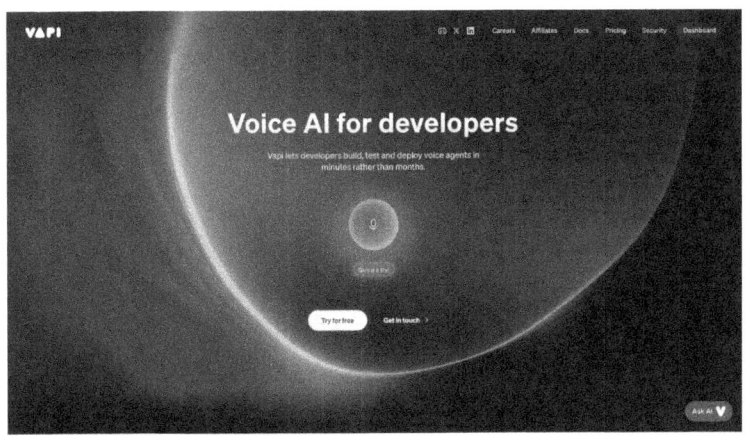

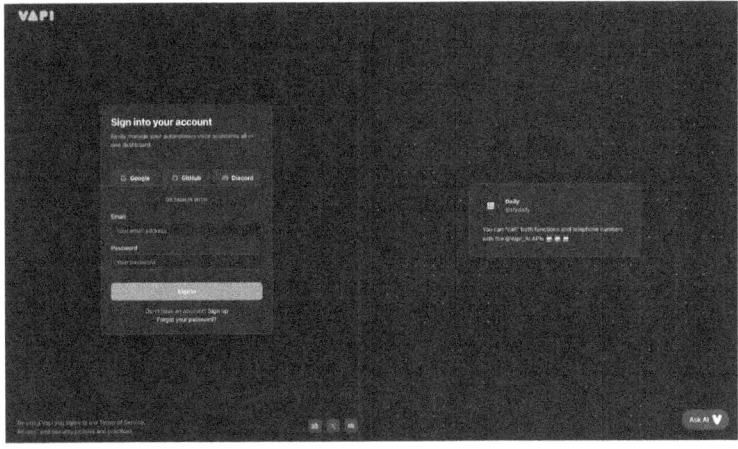

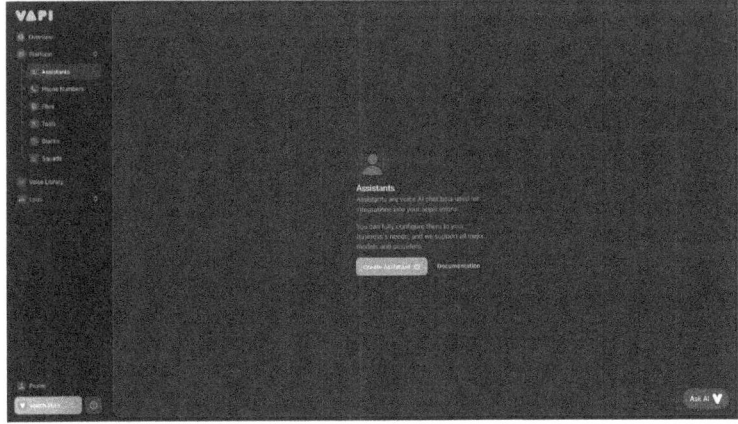

What You'll Need Before Starting

Make sure you have:

1. **An Account on Vapi.ai**: If you haven't signed up yet, we'll walk you through it shortly.
2. **Scripts from Chapter 3**: You should have already created scripts for different scenarios using ChatGPT. Have these ready on your computer.
3. **An Idea of Your Business's Needs**: Know what you want your AI assistant to do, such as booking appointments, answering questions, or transferring calls.

Step-by-Step Guide to Setting Up Your AI Voice Assistant

Let's break down the process into manageable steps.

Step 1: Signing Up for Vapi.ai

1. **Go to Vapi.ai**: Open your web browser and visit Vapi.ai.
2. **Create an Account**:
   - Click on the "Sign Up" button.
   - Enter your email address, create a password, and complete any other required fields.
   - Check your email for a verification link. Click on it to activate your account.
3. **Log In to Your Account**: Once your account is verified, log in using your email and password.

Tip: If Vapi.ai offers a free trial, start with that. It's a good way to experiment before committing to a paid plan.

Step 2: Creating a New Project

1. **Navigate to Your Dashboard**: Once logged in, you'll see your Vapi.ai dashboard. This is the main control center where you'll manage your AI assistants.
2. **Create a New Project**:
    - Click the "Create New Project" button.
    - Give your project a name, such as "AI Receptionist" or "Customer Support Assistant."
    - Select the type of assistant you want to create (e.g., voice assistant or chatbot). For our purposes, choose "Voice Assistant."
3. **Set Your Language and Region**: Choose the primary language your customers speak, such as English, and select the region if it applies (e.g., US English, UK English).

Step 3: Choosing a Voice for Your Assistant

Your AI assistant's voice is important because it sets the tone for customer interactions.

1. **Browse Voice Options**: Vapi.ai offers different voice profiles, such as male, female, formal, friendly, or even voices with regional accents.
2. **Listen to Samples**: Click on each voice option to hear a sample. Choose the one that best fits your brand. For example:
    - **Friendly and Warm**: Ideal for a family-friendly business, like a bakery or daycare.
    - **Professional and Calm**: Suitable for a law office or medical clinic
3. **Select Your Voice**: Once you've made your choice, save the settings.

Tip: If you're not sure which voice to pick, ask colleagues or friends for feedback.

Step 4: Uploading Your Scripts from ChatGPT

Now it's time to add the scripts you created in Chapter 3 to your AI assistant.

1. **Go to the Script Management Section**: Look for an option like "Manage Scripts" or "Add Scripts" in your Vapi.ai dashboard.
2. **Upload or Paste Your Scripts:**
    - Click "Add Script" and either paste your text or upload the file.
    - Label each script based on its purpose, such as "Greeting," "FAQ - Business Hours," or "Appointment Scheduling."
3. **Assign Scenarios to Each Script**:
    - In Vapi.ai, you'll see options to assign scripts to different scenarios. For example, you can set the "Greeting" script to play when a call is first answered.
    - If you have multiple scripts for the same type of interaction (e.g., different answers to FAQs), organize them so the AI knows when to use each one.

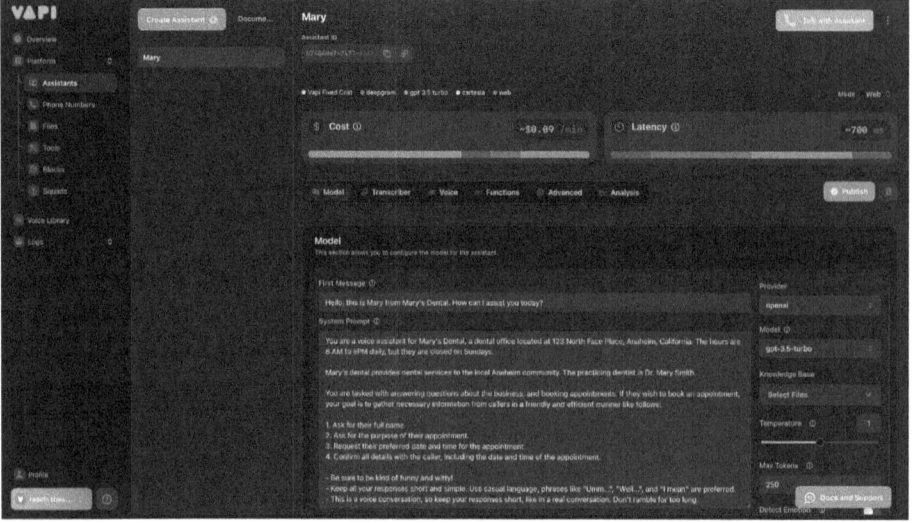

Example Setup:

- **Greeting Script**: Plays when the AI answers a call.
- **Appointment Booking Script**: Activates when a customer asks to schedule an appointment.
- **Complaint Handling Script**: Used when a customer expresses dissatisfaction.

Step 5: Configuring Your AI Assistant's Behavior
This step involves setting rules and actions for your assistant.

1. **Setting Up Call Handling**:
    - **Default Actions**: Decide what happens when the AI answers a call. For example, it could greet the caller and ask how it can help.
    - **Call Transfers**: Configure how and when the AI should transfer a call to a human employee. For example, if the AI can't answer a complex question, it could say, "Let me connect you to a human representative," and then transfer the call.
    - **Voicemail Setup**: If no human is available, the AI can take a voicemail. You can customize the voicemail script, such as, "I'm sorry, everyone is currently busy. Please leave a message, and we'll get back to you shortly."
2. **Adding Fallback Responses**:
    - Fallback responses are used when the AI doesn't understand what the customer is asking. For example: "I'm sorry, I didn't catch that. Could you please repeat your question?"
    - You can customize multiple fallback responses to make interactions feel less repetitive.

Tip: Keep fallback responses polite and helpful to maintain a positive experience for the customer.

Step 6: Testing Your AI Assistant

Before making your AI assistant live, you need to test it to make sure everything works as expected.

1. **Run Sample Calls**: Vapi.ai usually has a testing feature where you can simulate a call. Try out different scenarios, like booking an appointment or asking an FAQ.
2. **Check for Errors**: Does the AI respond correctly? Are the scripts triggering as expected? If something doesn't work, go back to the settings and make adjustments.
3. **Listen for Natural Flow**: Make sure the conversation sounds natural and that the voice you chose fits well with the content of your scripts.

Example Test Scenarios:

- Call the AI and pretend to be a customer asking about business hours.
- Try scheduling an appointment to see if the AI follows the script correctly.
- Ask a question the AI might not know and see how it handles the fallback response.

Step 7: Making Adjustments and Optimizing

Even if everything seems to be working, it's a good idea to make minor improvements based on your tests.

1. **Fine-Tune the Scripts**: If any part of the conversation sounds awkward, go back and edit the script. Use ChatGPT to rewrite or polish any parts that need improvement.
2. **Adjust Call Flow**: You might notice that certain scenarios need to be rearranged for better clarity. For example, if customers often ask follow-up questions after booking an appointment, prepare the AI to handle those.
3. **Review Voice Settings**: Make sure the chosen voice still feels right after testing. Sometimes, a different tone might work better based on feedback.

Step 8: Preparing for Launch

Once you're happy with your AI assistant, it's time to make it available to your customers.

1. **Set Live Hours**: Decide if the AI will be available 24/7 or only during specific hours. This is especially important if you want to forward calls to a human during business hours.
2. **Announce the AI to Your Team**: Let your staff know about the AI assistant and explain how it will help. Provide instructions on how to handle calls transferred by the AI.
3. **Inform Your Customers**: You can add a note on your website or social media, like, "We're excited to introduce our new AI assistant to help with your calls and questions. Available 24/7 for your convenience!"

Final Thoughts and Next Steps

Congratulations! You've successfully built and customized your AI voice assistant using Vapi.ai. But remember, this is just the beginning. Your assistant will get smarter and more effective over time as you make improvements and add new scripts.

In the Next Chapter: We'll dive into **Make.com** and learn how to automate workflows, such as syncing appointment bookings with your calendar and sending email confirmations to your clients. This will take your AI setup to the next level, making your operations even more efficient.

Let's keep building together and bring your AI assistant to life!

Chapter 5: Automating Workflows with Make.com

Welcome to Chapter 5! Now that you have your AI voice assistant set up with Vapi.ai, it's time to make your business processes even smoother and more efficient using **Make.com**. Make.com is a powerful tool that automates repetitive tasks and connects different apps and services seamlessly, reducing manual work and minimizing errors. Think of it as the glue that holds your digital operations together.

If you're not familiar with automation tools, don't worry! This chapter will guide you through everything step-by-step, so you can get the most out of your AI assistant and improve your workflow.

What Is Make.com and Why Do We Use It?

Make.com (formerly known as Integromat) is an online automation platform that connects various software applications. It enables you to create workflows (called *scenarios*) that automate tasks, like transferring data between apps, sending notifications, or updating records.

Why Use Make.com?

- **Automate Repetitive Tasks**: Free up time and resources by automating things like appointment scheduling, email notifications, or data logging.
- **Improve Accuracy**: Automation reduces the chances of human error, ensuring tasks are completed consistently and reliably.
- **Connect Multiple Apps**: Make.com works with many popular tools, like Google Calendar, Gmail, Vapi.ai, and CRM systems, allowing seamless data flow across your business.

What You'll Need Before Starting

- **A Make.com Account**: You'll need to sign up for Make.com. We'll walk you through it shortly.
- **Access to Your Vapi.ai Project**: Make sure you're logged into Vapi.ai so you can connect it to Make.com.
- **Other Tools You Use**: If you plan to automate tasks involving apps like Google Calendar, Gmail, or your CRM, have those accounts ready as well.

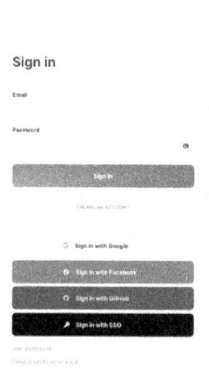

Step-by-Step Guide to Setting Up Automation with make.com

Let's get into the nitty-gritty of using Make.com. We'll break down the process into easy-to-follow steps

Step 1: Signing Up for make.com

1. **Go to Make.com**: Open your browser and visit Make.com.
2. **Create an Account**:
   - Click on the "Sign Up" button.
   - Enter your email address, create a password, and complete any required verification steps.
   - Alternatively, you can sign up using your Google or Facebook account.
3. **Explore the Dashboard**: Once logged in, you'll see the Make.com dashboard. This is where you'll create and manage your automation workflows.

Tip: Make.com offers a free plan with limited features, which is perfect for trying things out before upgrading if needed.

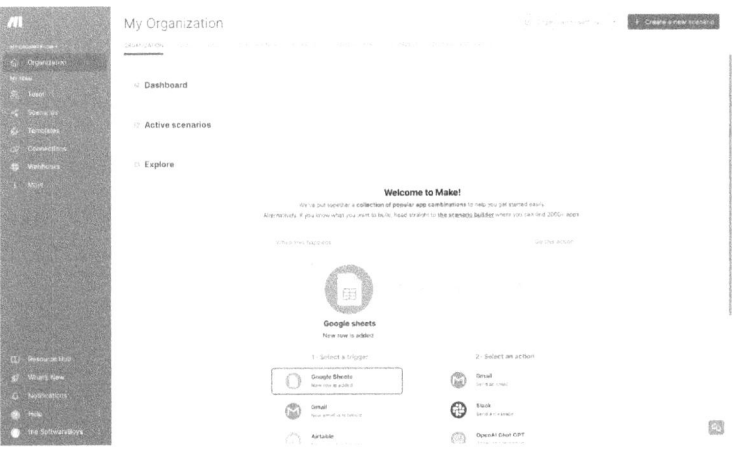

Step 2: Understanding the Make.com Interface

Before we create our first workflow, let's get familiar with the Make.com interface.

1. **Dashboard**: This is your main hub, where you can see all your workflows (scenarios) and manage your account settings.
2. **Scenarios**: In Make.com, automation workflows are called *scenarios*. Each scenario is a series of steps that automate a specific task or process.
3. **Modules**: Modules are the building blocks of your scenarios. Each module represents an action, like "send an email" or "add an event to Google Calendar."

Example: If you want to automate appointment scheduling, your scenario might have modules that connect Vapi.ai to Google Calendar and then send a confirmation email.

Step 3: Creating Your First Scenario

Let's create a simple automation workflow to connect your AI voice assistant with Google Calendar, so appointments booked by the AI are automatically added to your calendar.

Scenario: Automate Appointment Booking with Google Calendar

Goal: When a customer books an appointment using your AI assistant, Make.com will automatically add the appointment to your Google Calendar.

Step 3.1: Setting Up the Scenario

1. **Click "Create New Scenario"**: This button is usually at the top right of your dashboard.
2. **Choose a Trigger Module**:
   - **What's a Trigger?**: A trigger is the event that starts your workflow. In this case, the trigger will be when the AI assistant confirms an appointment.
   - **Select Vapi.ai**: Search for and select Vapi.ai as your trigger app. If it's not in the default list, use the search bar to find it.
   - **Choose the Trigger Event**: Select an event like "New Appointment Booked" or "Call Completed" (depending on how your AI assistant is set up).

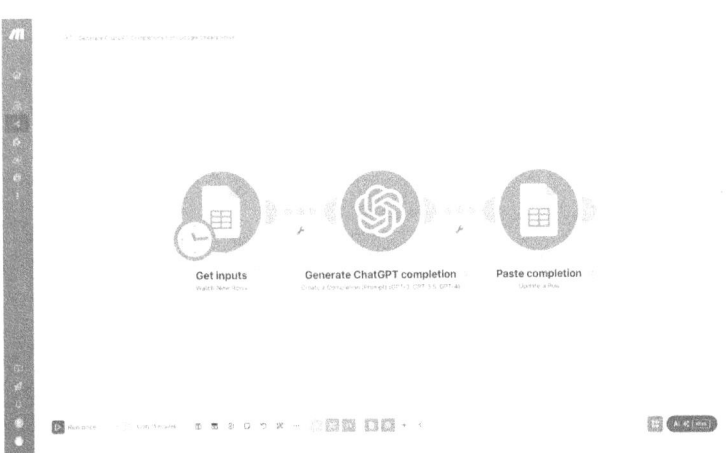

Step 3.2: Configuring the Trigger

1. **Connect Vapi.ai to Make.com**:
    - You'll be prompted to connect your Vapi.ai account. Click on "Add" and enter your Vapi.ai API key (you can find this in your Vapi.ai account settings).
2. **Set Trigger Details**:
    - Specify any filters or conditions, like only triggering for certain appointment types or specific days of the week.
    - **Example**: If you only want to add appointments for consultations, you can filter by the appointment type.

Step 4: Adding an Action Module (Google Calendar)

Now that we have our trigger set up, we need to tell Make.com what to do when an appointment is booked.

1. **Add a Google Calendar Module**:
    - Click on the plus sign (+) to add a new module.
    - Search for "Google Calendar" and select it.
2. **Choose the Action**: Select "Create an Event" as the action.
3. **Connect Your Google Calendar**:
    - Click "Add" to connect your Google account. You'll need to grant Make.com permission to access your calendar.
4. **Configure the Event Details**:
    - **Title**: Use a dynamic field to insert the customer's name or purpose of the appointment (e.g., "Consultation with John Doe").
    - **Date and Time**: Map these fields to the appointment details provided by Vapi.ai.
    - **Description**: Include additional information, like customer notes or contact details.

Tip: Use placeholders or variables from Vapi.ai to personalize the calendar event.

Step 5: Adding Additional Actions (Email Notification)

Let's make the scenario even more useful by adding an email notification to confirm the appointment with the customer.

1. **Add a Gmail Module**:
    - Click the plus sign (+) to add another module.
    - Search for "Gmail" (or any email service you use) and select it.
2. **Choose the Action**: Select "Send an Email."
3. **Connect Your Email Account**:
    - Click "Add" to connect your email account. Follow the prompts to authorize Make.com.
4. **Compose the Email**:
    - **To**: Use a dynamic field to insert the customer's email address.
    - **Subject**: "Appointment Confirmation with [Your Business Name]"
    - **Body**: Include details like the appointment date, time, and location, along with a friendly message.
    - **Example**: "Dear [Customer Name], your appointment has been scheduled for [Date & Time]. If you have any questions, feel free to contact us. We look forward to seeing you!"

Step 6: Testing Your Scenario

Before going live, it's essential to test your scenario to make sure everything works correctly.

1. **Click "Run Once"**: This option lets you test your scenario manually.
2. **Simulate an Appointment Booking**: Either have a colleague use the AI assistant or simulate the event in Vapi.ai.
3. **Check Your Google Calendar**: Make sure the event was added correctly, with all the details in place.
4. **Check Your Email**: Verify that the confirmation email was sent to the customer.

Troubleshooting Tips:

- **Error Messages**: If something doesn't work, check for error messages in Make.com and follow the suggested fixes.
- **Data Mapping Issues**: Make sure you're correctly mapping fields from Vapi.ai to Google Calendar and Gmail.

Step 7: Activating Your Scenario

Once everything works as expected, it's time to activate your scenario so it runs automatically.

1. **Click "Activate"**: Your scenario will now run in the background whenever the trigger event occurs.
2. **Set a Schedule**: You can choose how often Make.com checks for trigger events, such as "every 5 minutes" or "immediately."

Other Useful Automation Ideas

1. **Follow-Up Reminders**: Create a scenario that sends a reminder email or SMS to customers 24 hours before their appointment.
2. **Data Logging**: Automatically log customer interactions in a Google Sheet or your CRM for easy tracking and analysis.
3. **Slack Notifications for Your Team**: If you use Slack, set up a notification that alerts your team whenever a new appointment is booked or a voicemail is left.

Step 8: Optimizing and Expanding Your Workflows

1. **Monitor Performance**: Regularly check Make.com to ensure your scenarios are running smoothly. Look for any errors or delays.
2. **Add More Scenarios**: As you become more comfortable, add more automation to streamline other parts of your business, like sending follow-up emails to leads or updating inventory records.
3. **Review and Refine**: Automation is all about continuous improvement. Adjust your workflows based on customer feedback and business needs.

Final Thoughts

Congratulations! You've now successfully set up automation workflows using Make.com. These workflows will help your AI voice assistant run smoothly and efficiently, saving you time and improving your customer experience.

In the next chapter, we'll explore setting up telephony features with **Twilio** to enable your AI assistant to handle real phone calls and SMS messages. Let's keep the momentum going and continue building your smart, automated business solution!

Chapter 6: Adding Telephony Features with Twilio

Welcome to Chapter 6! Now that we have our AI assistant set up and workflows automated using Make.com, the next step is to enable phone and SMS communication. This is where **Twilio** comes in.

Twilio is a cloud-based communication platform that allows your AI voice assistant to make and receive phone calls, as well as send and receive SMS messages. If you're new to telephony or have no idea how this works, don't worry. We'll walk you through every step in a simple and easy-to-understand way.

What Is Twilio and Why Do We Use It?

Twilio is a service that lets businesses build communication features into their applications. It's widely used for things like automated calls, text message notifications, and two-factor authentication. In our case, we'll use Twilio to give our AI voice assistant the ability to interact with customers over the phone and through SMS.

Why Use Twilio?

- **Reliable**: Twilio has a proven track record of handling millions of calls and texts daily, making it a reliable choice for your business.
- **Scalable**: Whether your business handles a few calls a day or thousands, Twilio can scale to meet your needs.
- **Easy Integration**: Twilio works well with platforms like Vapi.ai and Make.com, allowing seamless setup.

What You'll Need Before Starting

- **A Twilio Account**: You'll need to sign up for Twilio. We'll guide you through this process.
- **Your Vapi.ai Project**: Make sure you have access to your Vapi.ai account so you can connect it to Twilio.
- **A Basic Understanding of Your Communication Needs**: Think about how you want to use phone and SMS features. Do you need to send appointment reminders, handle incoming calls, or send follow-up texts?

Step-by-Step Guide to Setting Up Twilio

Let's get started with setting up Twilio. This step-by-step guide will help you configure your account, get a phone number, and integrate Twilio with your AI assistant.

Step 1: Signing Up for Twilio

1. **Go to Twilio's Website**: Open your browser and visit Twilio.
2. **Create an Account**:
   - Click on the "Sign Up" button.
   - Enter your email address, create a password, and follow the prompts to complete the registration process.
   - You'll be asked to verify your email and phone number. Follow the instructions to do so.
3. **Choose a Free Trial (if available)**: Twilio offers a free trial with a small amount of credit. This is perfect for testing out features before committing to a paid plan.

Tip: During sign-up, Twilio may ask you how you plan to use their service. You can select options like "Send and receive SMS" or "Make and receive phone calls" based on your needs.

Step 2: Getting a Twilio Phone Number

To enable phone and SMS features, you'll need to get a Twilio phone number.

1. **Log In to Your Twilio Dashboard**: Once you've signed up and logged in, you'll see your Twilio Console (dashboard).
2. **Navigate to "Phone Numbers"**:
   - Click on "Phone Numbers" in the left-hand menu.
   - Click on "Buy a Number."
3. **Choose Your Phone Number**:
   - Twilio will show you a list of available phone numbers. You can filter by country, area code, or capabilities (e.g., SMS, voice, or both).
   - Choose a number that meets your needs and click "Buy."
   - **Note**: If you're using the free trial, you may be limited to certain numbers.

Step 3: Configuring Your Twilio Phone Number

Now that you have a phone number, let's configure it to handle voice calls and SMS messages.

1. **Click on Your Phone Number**: In the "Phone Numbers" section of your dashboard, click on the number you just purchased.
2. **Set Up Voice and SMS Webhooks**:
   - **Voice**: Under the "Voice & Fax" section, you'll see options for handling incoming calls. You'll need to set a "Webhook" URL where Twilio will send call information. This URL will come from your Vapi.ai project (we'll cover this shortly).
   - **SMS**: Similarly, in the "Messaging" section, set a Webhook URL to handle incoming text messages. This will also be provided by Vapi.ai if you plan to use SMS features.
3. **Save Your Settings**: Once everything is configured, click "Save."

What's a Webhook?

- A **Webhook** is a URL that receives data from another service.

  In our case, it's how Twilio sends call and message details to Vapi.ai so the AI assistant can handle them.

Step 4: Connecting Twilio to Vapi.ai

1. **Log In to Vapi.ai**: Open a new tab and log in to your Vapi.ai account.
2. **Navigate to "Telephony Settings"**:
   - Find the section in your project settings for telephony or integrations.
3. **Select Twilio as Your Provider**:
   - You'll see options for telephony providers. Choose "Twilio."
4. **Enter Your Twilio Credentials**:
   - You'll need your Twilio **Account SID** and **Auth Token**. These can be found on your Twilio Console (dashboard).
   - Copy and paste these credentials into Vapi.ai to link your accounts.
5. **Set Up Webhooks in Vapi.ai**:
   - Vapi.ai will generate Webhook URLs for handling voice calls and SMS. Copy these URLs and go back to your Twilio dashboard to paste them in the appropriate fields.
   - **Voice Webhook**: Paste this URL in the "Voice & Fax" section in Twilio.
   - **SMS Webhook**: Paste this URL in the "Messaging" section in Twilio.
6. **Save and Test the Integration**: Make sure to save all settings. You can now test the integration by making a test call or sending a test SMS to see if everything works.

Step 5: Configuring Call and SMS Handling in Vapi.ai

1. **Setting Up Call Flows**:
    - Go back to your Vapi.ai dashboard and configure how your AI assistant should handle incoming calls.
    - **Greeting**: Choose the greeting script you uploaded earlier. For example, "Hello! You've reached [Your Business Name]. How can I assist you today?"
    - **Call Routing**: Decide if and when calls should be forwarded to a human. For instance, you might want to forward calls only if the customer has a complex request the AI can't handle.
    - **Voicemail**: Set up a voicemail script for when no one is available. For example, "I'm sorry, all representatives are currently busy. Please leave a message, and we'll get back to you soon."
2. **Setting Up SMS Responses**:
    - If you plan to use SMS, configure how your AI assistant should respond to text messages.
    - **Automatic Replies**: For common questions, you can set up automatic SMS responses. For example, if someone texts "What are your hours?" the AI can reply, "Our business hours are Monday to Friday, 9 AM to 5 PM."

Step 6: Testing Your Twilio Integration

It's crucial to test everything to ensure it's working as expected.

1. **Make a Test Call**: Use your mobile phone to call the Twilio number you set up. The AI assistant should answer and follow the script you configured in Vapi.ai.
    - **Test Different Scenarios**: Try asking questions or making requests to see how the AI responds.
    - **Check Call Forwarding**: If you set up call forwarding, make sure the call is transferred to a human when needed.

2. **Send a Test SMS**: Text the Twilio number from your phone and see if the AI responds correctly.
   - **Check for Delays**: Make sure there are no significant delays in the response.

Troubleshooting Tips:

- **No Response from the AI**: Double-check your Webhook URLs in Twilio and make sure they match what's provided by Vapi.ai.
- **Call Quality Issues**: Ensure your internet connection is stable and that there are no restrictions on the Twilio side.

Step 7: Going Live

Once you're confident everything works correctly, you can make your AI assistant available to the public.

1. **Activate Your Twilio Number**: If you were using a free trial number, consider upgrading to a paid number to remove any trial limitations.
2. **Announce the New Feature to Your Customers**: Let your customers know that they can now call or text your business 24/7 and interact with your AI assistant.
   - You can update your website, social media, or send an email announcement.

Step 8: Using Twilio for Outbound Calls and SMS

Twilio isn't just for incoming communication. You can also use it to make outbound calls or send SMS notifications.

1. **Setting Up Outbound Calls**:
   - Configure Vapi.ai to make outbound calls, like appointment reminders or follow-ups. You'll need to set up scripts for these scenarios in Vapi.ai.
2. **Sending SMS Reminders**:
   - Use Twilio to send automated SMS reminders for appointments. For example, "Hi [Customer Name], this is a reminder for your appointment at [Time]. Reply 'YES' to confirm or 'RESCHEDULE' to change the time."

Example Use Case:

- **Appointment Reminder Workflow**:
  - When an appointment is booked, Vapi.ai triggers an SMS reminder using Twilio.
  - If the customer replies "RESCHEDULE," the AI assistant can guide them through the rescheduling process

Final Thoughts

You've now successfully set up Twilio and integrated it with your AI voice assistant! With this setup, your business is ready to handle phone and SMS communication efficiently and professionally. Remember, you can always expand your setup by adding more features or refining your scripts based on customer feedback.

In the Next Chapter: We'll explore real-world use cases and best practices to help you optimize your AI voice solution for maximum impact. You'll learn how businesses like yours are using these tools to transform their operations.

Let's keep moving forward and make the most of your AI-powered communication system!

Chapter 7: Putting It All Together – Integrating and Optimizing Your AI Voice Solution

Congratulations on making it this far! You've set up ChatGPT for voice prompts, configured your AI assistant with Vapi.ai, automated workflows using Make.com, and added telephony features with Twilio. Now it's time to connect everything into a seamless, efficient, and fully functional AI voice system. This chapter will guide you step-by-step to integrate all the components, test the complete system, and optimize your AI solution for the best possible performance.

What Does "Putting It All Together" Mean?

In simple terms, this chapter is about making sure your AI voice assistant operates smoothly and effectively across all platforms. We'll ensure that when a customer calls, your AI assistant answers correctly, schedules appointments using automation, sends confirmation messages, and seamlessly transfers calls to a human when necessary. It's the final step to create a polished, automated communication solution for your business.

What You'll Need Before We Start

- **All Accounts Ready**: Ensure you have your ChatGPT scripts, Vapi.ai project, Make.com account, and Twilio setup all completed from previous chapters.
- **A Clear Understanding of Your Workflow**: Think about the flow of communication from start to finish. For example, a customer calls, speaks to the AI, schedules an appointment, and receives a confirmation email or SMS.

Step-by-Step Guide to Integrating Everything

Let's walk through the integration process from start to finish.

Step 1: Review Your Workflow

Before connecting everything, review the workflow you want to automate. Here's an example of a simple end-to-end workflow:

1. **Customer Calls Your Business**: The call is received by Twilio and directed to your AI assistant in Vapi.ai.
2. **AI Assistant Responds**: The AI answers the call, greets the customer, and handles the request (e.g., booking an appointment, answering FAQs, or transferring the call to a human).
3. **Automation Triggers**: If the customer books an appointment, Make.com automates the process, adding the event to your calendar and sending a confirmation message via Twilio.

4. **Follow-Up and Notifications**: Your AI system sends follow-up reminders or logs call details for future reference.

Write Down Your Workflow: Having a visual representation or a simple checklist of the process will help you during setup.

Step 2: Connecting Vapi.ai and Twilio

1. **Double-Check Your Webhook URLs**:
   - Go to your Twilio dashboard and ensure that the Webhook URLs from Vapi.ai are correctly entered for both voice and SMS handling.
   - **Voice Webhook**: This should be configured to direct incoming calls to your AI assistant in Vapi.ai.
   - **SMS Webhook**: This should handle incoming text messages and send them to Vapi.ai for processing.
2. **Test the Connection**:
   - Make a test call to your Twilio number and see if the AI assistant answers. If it does, ask it a few questions or try booking an appointment.
   - Send a test SMS to see if the AI assistant responds appropriately.

Troubleshooting Tips:

- If the AI doesn't respond correctly, check your Webhook URLs and API credentials in both Vapi.ai and Twilio.
- Make sure your Vapi.ai project is set to "Active" and is ready to handle incoming calls and messages.

Step 3: Integrating Vapi.ai with make.com

1. **Log In to Make.com**: Open your Make.com dashboard.
2. **Create a New Scenario for Automation**:
    - Click on "Create New Scenario."
3. **Set Up the Trigger**:
    - Choose Vapi.ai as your trigger app and select an event like "New Appointment Booked" or "Call Completed."
    - **Example Trigger**: "When an appointment is booked by the AI assistant, start the automation."
4. **Add Action Modules**:
    - **Google Calendar Module**: Add an event to your Google Calendar with details from the appointment.
        - **Title**: Use a dynamic field to insert the customer's name and the purpose of the appointment.
        - **Date and Time**: Map these fields from the Vapi.ai data.
    - **Gmail or Twilio SMS Module**: Send a confirmation message to the customer.
        - **Email**: Use Gmail to send an email confirmation.
        - **SMS**: Use Twilio to send a text message if the customer prefers SMS notifications.
5. **Map the Data**: Make sure you correctly map data from Vapi.ai to Google Calendar and your email/SMS service. For example:
    - **Customer Name**: From Vapi.ai → To Google Calendar or SMS.
    - **Appointment Time**: From Vapi.ai → To Google Calendar or SMS.

Testing the Automation:

- Run the scenario manually in Make.com to ensure everything is working as expected. Check that the appointment is added to your calendar and that the customer receives a confirmation message.

Step 4: Handling Call Transfers and Voicemail

1. **Configuring Call Transfers in Vapi.ai**:
    - If your AI assistant cannot handle a request, you can set up call transfers to a human representative.
    - **Example**: If a customer needs to speak to someone directly, the AI can say, "Let me transfer you to a human representative," and then forward the call using Twilio.
    - **Set Up Transfer Rules**: In Vapi.ai, define the scenarios where a transfer should occur and input the phone numbers for the human representatives.
2. **Setting Up Voicemail**:
    - If no one is available to take the call, configure a voicemail system.
    - **Voicemail Script**: Use a friendly and professional script, like, "I'm sorry, all our representatives are currently busy. Please leave a message with your name and phone number, and we'll get back to you shortly."
    - **Voicemail Handling**: You can use Twilio to send voicemail details to your email or log them in a spreadsheet using Make.com.

Testing Call Transfers and Voicemail:

- Simulate a situation where the AI cannot handle a request and see if the call is correctly transferred.
- Call during off-hours to ensure the voicemail system works and that messages are logged properly.

Step 5: End-to-End Testing

It's crucial to test the entire system to make sure everything works seamlessly.

1. **Simulate Different Scenarios**:
    - **Incoming Call**: Call your Twilio number and ask the AI to book an appointment. Check if the appointment is added to your calendar and if a confirmation message is sent.
    - **Incoming SMS**: Send a text message asking for business hours or another common question. Make sure the AI responds correctly.
    - **Complex Requests**: Try to ask questions that the AI might not know. See if the AI handles these gracefully and transfers the call if needed.
2. **Check for Errors or Delays**:
    - Make sure there are no significant delays in responses.
    - If any part of the system doesn't work, double-check your integrations and data mappings.

Step 6: Optimizing Your AI Voice Solution

Once your system is up and running, consider ways to optimize it for better performance and customer experience.

1. **Improve Script Responses**:
   - Based on customer interactions, refine your scripts in ChatGPT to make them clearer or more helpful.
   - **Example**: If customers frequently ask the same question, add a more detailed response to that query.
2. **Analyze Call and Message Data**:
   - Use Make.com to log call and message data in a Google Sheet or your CRM. Review this data regularly to understand common customer needs or identify issues.
   - **Example**: If you notice a lot of calls being transferred to humans, consider updating your AI scripts or adding more automated responses.
3. **Adjust Call Handling Settings**:
   - If call transfers are happening too frequently, fine-tune the AI's ability to handle complex requests.
   - If voicemail messages are too long or unclear, update your voicemail script for better clarity.

Regularly Review and Update: As your business grows or customer needs change, update your AI assistant, scripts, and automation workflows accordingly.

Step 7: Going Live and Monitoring Performance

Now that everything is set up and tested, you're ready to go live!

1. **Activate All Components**:
   - Make sure your Twilio phone number is active and that all your scenarios in Make.com are running.
   - Double-check that Vapi.ai is set to "Active" and ready to handle incoming calls and messages.
2. **Announce the Launch**: Let your customers know about your new AI assistant. You can update your website, send an email, or post on social media.
3. **Monitor Performance**:
   - Use Make.com and Vapi.ai to monitor performance metrics, like the number of calls handled, successful automations, and customer feedback.
   - Make adjustments as needed to improve the experience.

Common Challenges and How to Solve Them

1. **Integration Issues**:
   - If data isn't flowing correctly between Vapi.ai, Make.com, and Twilio, double-check your API keys and Webhook URLs.
2. **Call Quality Problems**:
   - Ensure your internet connection is stable and that Twilio's settings are configured correctly.
3. **Customer Complaints About the AI**:
   - If customers find the AI responses unhelpful, review and improve your scripts. Use ChatGPT to create more nuanced or detailed answers.

Pro Tip: Schedule regular "check-up" sessions to review and optimize your AI voice solution. This will ensure it continues to meet your business needs effectively.

Chapter 8: Real-World Use Cases and Best Practices

Welcome to Chapter 8! You've already taken significant steps to set up your AI voice assistant, but understanding how this technology can transform everyday operations in real-world scenarios is crucial. This chapter will walk you through highly detailed, practical examples of AI voice solutions in action, explain the best practices to optimize these systems, and provide easy-to-follow explanations to ensure everything makes sense—even if you're starting from scratch.

One of the featured use cases will focus on an AI Voicemail Replacement System that modernizes traditional voicemail processes and integrates seamlessly into your business operations.

Why Real-World Use Cases Are Important

Real-world use cases provide concrete examples of how AI technology can solve everyday business challenges.

They help you visualize how an AI voice assistant can be adapted to meet your needs, whether you run a small business, a professional service, or a large corporation.

We'll cover use cases that range from customer service to automated lead generation and voicemail management.

By the end of this chapter, you'll understand the possibilities and learn best practices for implementing and optimizing your AI solution.

Use Case 1: AI Receptionist for a Medical Clinic

Background

Imagine a busy medical clinic, bustling with activity from the moment the doors open until closing time. The front desk staff are juggling multiple responsibilities, from checking in patients and handling paperwork to answering a constant stream of phone calls. The clinic receives hundreds of calls each day from patients who need to book appointments, inquire about insurance coverage, request directions, or simply ask about the clinic's operating hours.

These calls often come in waves, with peak times in the morning when patients are eager to secure same-day appointments or around lunchtime when people are more available to call. Handling this volume of calls effectively is a monumental task, and despite the staff's best efforts, it becomes overwhelming. As a result, patients who call the clinic often face long hold times, leading to frustration and a perception that the clinic is disorganized or unresponsive.

What This Looks Like in Practice:

- **Long Hold Times**: A patient calling to book an appointment might be put on hold for several minutes, listening to repetitive hold music or automated messages. By the time someone finally answers, the patient is often irritated and impatient.
- **Missed Calls**: During particularly busy times, calls may go unanswered or even be dropped, resulting in lost opportunities to serve patients who may need urgent care or information.
- **Staff Distraction**: The front desk staff are continuously interrupted by phone calls, making it difficult to give their full attention to in-person patients. This leads to errors, longer wait times for people standing in line, and an overall decline in service quality

Problem

The core issue is that the clinic's front desk staff are overburdened. They are stretched thin trying to balance the needs of in-person patients with those of callers. The constant interruption from phone calls makes it nearly impossible to manage other critical tasks effectively. For instance:

- **In-Person Patient Care Suffers**: When staff are tied up on the phone, patients standing in line to check in or ask questions are left waiting, which can negatively impact their experience. Staff members may also become frazzled, increasing the risk of errors, such as misplacing documents or double-booking appointments.

- **High Stress Levels Among Staff**: The front desk staff face constant pressure to manage all these tasks simultaneously, leading to burnout and reduced job satisfaction. This high-stress environment can also contribute to high staff turnover, which disrupts the clinic's operations even further.

- **Frustrated Patients and Missed Opportunities**: Long hold times mean that some patients may hang up before they get the information or assistance they need. This can result in missed opportunities for scheduling new appointments or addressing urgent medical concerns. Patients who experience this frustration may also leave negative reviews or choose to go to a different clinic in the future.

The AI Solution

To address these challenges, the clinic implemented an AI receptionist using Vapi.ai for voice communication, Make.com for workflow automation, and Twilio for handling phone call management. This solution transformed the clinic's operations and provided immediate relief for both staff and patients. Here's how the system works in detail:

- **Vapi.ai for Voice Communication**: The AI receptionist answers incoming calls and engages with patients using natural, conversational language. It's capable of understanding a wide range of patient requests, from booking appointments to providing office hours and answering questions about insurance. The AI uses Natural Language Processing (NLP) to accurately interpret what the caller needs and respond accordingly.

- **Make.com for Workflow Automation**: Once the AI identifies the caller's request, it uses Make.com to automate routine tasks. For example, if a patient wants to book an appointment, the AI seamlessly connects to the clinic's scheduling system, checks availability, and confirms the booking—all without human intervention. This automation not only saves time but also reduces the likelihood of errors in scheduling.

- **Twilio for Phone Call Management**: Twilio is used to manage the technical aspects of call handling, such as routing calls to the AI receptionist and transferring them to human staff when necessary. Twilio ensures that the call quality remains high and that calls are correctly directed, whether they are handled by the AI or need to be escalated to a human receptionist.

How This Solution Transforms the Clinic

1. **Immediate Call Handling**: The AI receptionist answers calls instantly, even during peak hours, eliminating the need for patients to wait on hold. This alone significantly improves the patient experience and reduces frustration.

2. **Efficient Task Management**: The AI takes over routine tasks, like scheduling appointments and providing basic information, freeing up front desk staff to focus on in-person patients and more complex administrative duties. Staff can now work more efficiently and provide higher-quality service to those physically present at the clinic.

3. **Stress Reduction for Staff**: With fewer interruptions from phone calls, the front desk staff experience less stress and can complete their work with greater accuracy and satisfaction. This leads to a more positive work environment and can reduce turnover rates.

4. **Improved Patient Satisfaction**: Patients benefit from a smoother, more efficient process when calling the clinic. They can easily book appointments, get answers to their questions, or be directed to the right resources without the frustration of long hold times. This leads to higher patient satisfaction and a better overall reputation for the clinic.

This AI solution represents a modern, efficient way to handle high call volumes in a medical setting, making life easier for both staff and patients while ensuring that the clinic operates smoothly and effectively.

Detailed Workflow

1. Greeting and Call Handling

- **Immediate Answer**: When a patient calls, the AI receptionist responds right away, even during busy periods, ensuring that no caller is left waiting.

- **AI Greeting**: The AI delivers a warm, professional message, such as: "Welcome to [Clinic Name]. How can I assist you today? You can say things like 'book an appointment,' 'ask about insurance,' or 'get directions.'"

- **Natural Language Understanding (NLU)**: Using advanced Natural Language Processing (NLP), the AI interprets the caller's request, whether it involves scheduling an appointment, asking about insurance, or requesting other clinic information.

2. Appointment Scheduling:

- **Real-Time Integration**: The AI integrates with the clinic's scheduling system through Make.com for up-to-the-minute schedule updates.

- **Booking Process**: If the patient wants to schedule an appointment, the AI checks the availability, confirms the details, and books the appointment.

- **Confirmation**: The AI sends a confirmation SMS or email to the patient, summarizing the appointment details and including a calendar link for convenience.

- **Automation**: Make.com ensures that all data is automatically updated, eliminating manual entry errors.

3. Handling Insurance Inquiries

Addressing Common Questions

The AI receptionist is pre-trained with a comprehensive understanding of the clinic's insurance policies and coverage details. It can instantly respond to frequently asked questions such as:

- **"Do you accept [specific insurance provider]?"** The AI can provide a list of accepted insurance providers and confirm coverage for the caller.
- **"What types of procedures are covered under my insurance?"** The AI can outline the general coverage for common procedures, such as routine check-ups, lab tests, or specialized treatments.
- **"How does billing work with my insurance?"** The AI explains the clinic's billing process, including whether co-pays are required upfront and how insurance claims are processed.

Fallback to a Human Staff Member

While the AI is equipped to handle a wide range of insurance-related questions, it recognizes when a query is too complex or requires detailed, case-specific information. For example:

- If a patient has a unique insurance plan with specific coverage nuances.
- When the caller needs a detailed breakdown of out-of-pocket costs for a planned procedure.

In these cases, the AI politely offers to transfer the call to a knowledgeable human staff member. The handoff is smooth, with the AI providing the staff member with a brief summary of the caller's inquiry, so the patient doesn't have to repeat themselves. This ensures a seamless experience while maintaining efficiency.

4. Call Routing and Escalation

Smart Call Transfer

The AI receptionist is designed to handle routine queries and tasks independently, but it also recognizes situations where human intervention is necessary. When an issue arises that requires the expertise or decision-making ability of a human staff member, the AI uses **smart call transfer** features to seamlessly connect the caller to the front desk or an appropriate department. Here's how it works in detail:

- **Automatic Transfer**: The AI identifies when a caller's request goes beyond its capabilities, such as specific questions about medical procedures or a detailed billing inquiry that requires access to confidential patient records.

- **Providing Context**: Before transferring the call, the AI gives the human staff member a brief summary of the caller's needs.

- For instance, if a patient asks about an upcoming surgical procedure, the AI informs the staff member: "The caller is asking for detailed information about their scheduled surgery and wants to discuss pre-operative instructions." This ensures that the staff member is well-prepared and can assist the caller efficiently without needing to ask for background information.

Priority Handling

The AI receptionist is programmed to recognize and prioritize urgent or emergency-related calls. When a caller mentions key phrases or describes a situation that indicates urgency, the AI acts immediately to ensure the call is escalated to the right person. Here's how it manages priority situations:

- **Emergency Detection**: The AI uses Natural Language Processing (NLP) to detect words and phrases like "emergency," "severe pain," "urgent," or "life-threatening." If the caller describes symptoms or situations that could be critical, the AI flags the call as high-priority.

- **Immediate Transfer**: Once the AI identifies the call as urgent, it bypasses all other processes and connects the caller to a human staff member or medical professional without delay. The AI also provides an alert to the staff, emphasizing the urgency of the situation.

- **Emergency Protocols**: In some cases, the AI may advise the caller to hang up and dial emergency services (such as 911) if the situation sounds life-threatening. For example, it might say: "This sounds like an emergency. Please hang up and call 911 for immediate assistance."

These features ensure that calls are directed to the appropriate person quickly and efficiently, reducing response times for critical situations and improving the overall patient experience.

5. Voicemail System for After-Hours Calls

AI-Managed Voicemail
When the clinic is closed, the AI voicemail system takes over seamlessly to ensure that no important message goes unheard or unattended. Here's a detailed look at how it works:

- **Friendly and Informative Prompt**: The AI greets after-hours callers with a warm and professional message, such as: "Thank you for calling [Clinic Name]. Our office is currently closed. Please leave your name, phone number, and a brief message, and we'll get back to you as soon as possible. If this is an emergency, please hang up and call 911."

- **Real-Time Transcription**: As the caller leaves their message, the AI transcribes the voicemail in real time. This means the spoken words are instantly converted into text, ensuring the content is captured accurately and efficiently. The transcription is detailed and includes all the critical information provided by the caller, such as:
    - **Caller's Name**: "Hi, this is Sarah Johnson..."
    - **Contact Information**: "...you can reach me at 555-123-4567..."
    - **Reason for the Call**: "...I'm calling to ask about my test results and discuss some severe pain I've been experiencing."

- **Automated Email Notification**: Once the voicemail is transcribed, the AI system sends an email to the clinic staff with the complete transcription and a summary of the message. The email includes:
    - **The Full Transcription**: A word-for-word text version of the caller's message for easy reference.
    - **The Caller's Contact Details**: The phone number and any other relevant contact information provided.

- ○ **The Original Audio File**: A link to the audio recording, so staff can listen to the message if needed for additional context.

- **Organized Documentation**: The AI saves the transcribed messages in a digital format, making it easy for the clinic to archive, search, and manage voicemails. This organized approach ensures that no message gets lost or overlooked.

Prioritization of Urgent Messages

The AI voicemail system is designed not only to transcribe messages but also to identify and flag urgent or high-priority communications. Here's how it handles these situations:

- **Keyword Detection**: The AI uses advanced Natural Language Processing (NLP) to scan the voicemail for specific words and phrases that indicate urgency. Examples include "urgent," "emergency," "severe pain," or "critical condition." If the caller mentions any of these keywords, the AI recognizes the need for immediate attention.

- **Priority Flagging**: Messages containing these keywords are automatically flagged and marked as urgent. In the email sent to the clinic staff, the subject line might include a notice like "Urgent: Immediate Attention Required" to ensure it stands out.

- **Highlighting Critical Details**: The email or notification will highlight the parts of the message that contain urgent keywords, making it easier for the clinic staff to assess the situation quickly. For example, if a caller says, "I'm experiencing severe chest pain," the AI will emphasize "severe chest pain" in the transcription.

- **Escalation Procedures**: The clinic can set up specific escalation protocols for flagged messages. For instance, an on-call physician may receive an SMS alert or a direct phone call if a message is marked as a true medical emergency. This ensures that critical issues are addressed immediately, even outside regular office hours.

- **Patient Reassurance**: By efficiently handling and prioritizing messages, the clinic ensures patients feel reassured that their concerns will be taken seriously and addressed promptly.

Benefits of the AI-Managed Voicemail System

1. **Efficiency**: Staff no longer have to sift through hours of voicemails manually. They can quickly read transcriptions, prioritize responses, and spend more time on patient care.

2. **Reduced Human Error**: The AI system minimizes the risk of missing important messages, as every voicemail is transcribed, documented, and flagged if necessary.

3. **Quick Access to Information**: Staff have instant access to the voicemail content, allowing them to prepare before calling patients back, which improves the quality of service.

4. **Enhanced Urgent Care**: By flagging critical messages and notifying the appropriate staff immediately, the clinic can ensure that urgent medical situations are handled with the urgency they require.

This AI voicemail system significantly streamlines communication for after-hours calls, ensuring that patients' needs are addressed efficiently and effectively, even when the clinic is closed.

6. Benefits and Results

Implementing an AI voice assistant in a medical clinic brings significant advantages that directly impact the clinic's workflow and the patient experience. Here's an in-depth look at these benefits:

1. Reduced Hold Times

- **Simultaneous Call Handling**: Traditional phone systems limit the number of incoming calls that can be answered at once. When the front desk staff are busy, calls are put on hold, often leading to long wait times. The AI voice assistant, however, can manage multiple calls simultaneously. This means that whether there are two or twenty people calling at the same time, the AI can answer each one instantly without making anyone wait.

- **No More Waiting in Line**: Patients no longer have to listen to hold music or automated messages about their position in the queue. The AI immediately engages with each caller, offering assistance right away. This is particularly beneficial during peak hours, such as early mornings or around lunchtime, when call volumes are highest.

- **Efficient Use of Call Time**: The AI quickly identifies the caller's needs—whether it's scheduling an appointment, checking insurance coverage, or providing office hours information—without the typical delays that come with human call handling. This efficiency not only saves time for the caller but also streamlines the clinic's phone operations.

Impact: By eliminating long hold times, the AI voice assistant greatly improves the overall phone experience for patients. This reduction in wait times can lead to fewer hang-ups or abandoned calls, which means more patients get the assistance they need when they need it.

2. Increased Efficiency

- **Focus on In-Person Interactions**: Front desk staff are often the first point of contact for patients arriving at the clinic. With the constant distraction of answering phone calls, staff may find it challenging to give their full attention to patients who are checking in, filling out forms, or asking questions. The AI assistant alleviates this burden by taking over routine phone tasks, allowing staff to focus on providing quality, face-to-face service to patients in the clinic.

- **Reduced Task Overload**: In a busy clinic, front desk staff are responsible for a variety of tasks, from managing appointments and updating patient records to assisting with billing inquiries and administrative work. By automating phone calls, the AI system reduces the workload, freeing up staff to complete their duties more efficiently. This leads to fewer errors and a smoother operation overall.

- **Streamlined Workflow**: The AI can handle repetitive inquiries, such as office hours or appointment scheduling, without human intervention. This automation ensures that staff members are only involved in tasks that require their expertise, such as addressing complex patient questions or handling sensitive medical information.

Impact: The increased efficiency leads to a more organized and less stressful work environment for staff. It also boosts productivity, as employees are better able to manage their responsibilities without feeling overwhelmed by phone calls.

3. Improved Patient Satisfaction

- **Smoother Appointment Booking**: One of the most common reasons patients call a clinic is to schedule or reschedule appointments. The AI assistant simplifies this process by offering a clear and intuitive booking system. Patients can easily state their preferred date and time, and the AI checks the clinic's calendar for availability. If the desired slot is not available, the AI can offer alternative times, making the experience as smooth as possible.

- **Accurate Information Delivery**: The AI is trained to provide up-to-date and accurate information about the clinic's services, office hours, and accepted insurance plans. This ensures that patients receive reliable answers, which builds trust in the clinic's operations. If a patient asks about a procedure or coverage, they can feel confident that the information provided by the AI is correct.

- **24/7 Availability**: Even when the clinic is closed, the AI voice assistant is available to answer calls, take messages, and provide essential information. Patients appreciate the convenience of being able to get answers or leave a message at any time, which enhances their overall experience with the clinic.

- **Personalized Interactions**: Although the AI is not human, it can be programmed to deliver responses in a warm, empathetic tone, making interactions feel more personal and considerate. For example, the AI can express concern when a patient mentions feeling unwell or offer a friendly farewell at the end of a call.

Impact: By providing a faster, more efficient, and user-friendly experience, the AI voice assistant significantly improves patient satisfaction. Patients are more likely to have a positive impression of the clinic, recommend it to others, and return for future care. Additionally, the clinic benefits from better patient retention and a strong reputation in the community.

Overall Impact on the Clinic

The combination of reduced hold times, increased efficiency, and improved patient satisfaction creates a more streamlined and effective clinic environment. Staff are less stressed, patients are happier, and the clinic can operate more smoothly, even during the busiest times. The AI voice assistant serves as a valuable tool, enhancing both the patient and staff experience in a meaningful way.

Use Case 2: AI Customer Service Agent for an E-commerce Store

Background

Imagine an online retailer that specializes in selling home goods such as furniture, décor, kitchenware, and bedding. This retailer is known for offering high-quality products and frequently holds major sales events that attract a large number of shoppers. Events like **Black Friday**, **holiday promotions**, and **end-of-season clearance sales** are particularly popular, drawing in thousands of potential customers looking to take advantage of limited-time discounts.

During these peak sales periods, the retailer's website sees a significant uptick in traffic. Shoppers are eager to make informed purchasing decisions, so they reach out to the store's customer service team with a flood of inquiries. These questions typically revolve around:

- **Product Features**: Customers want to know specifics about the materials, dimensions, durability, or color options of a particular product before making a purchase. For example, "Is this sofa made of genuine leather, and does it come in a lighter shade of grey?"

- **Shipping Timelines**: With the excitement of sales events, many customers want to know exactly when their items will arrive. Questions like "If I order today, will I receive my package by Christmas?" are extremely common.

- **Return Policies**: Shoppers also want clarity on how returns are handled, especially for large items like furniture. Questions may include, "What's your return policy for a dining table if it arrives damaged?"

The result is an overwhelming surge in customer service inquiries that come in through various channels, including phone calls, emails, live chat, and SMS. The support team, which is relatively small and operates with a limited number of agents, struggles to keep up with this influx of questions.

Problem

Despite working tirelessly, the customer service team finds it challenging to maintain quick response times when sales events create an avalanche of inquiries. This delay in responding has several negative consequences:

1. **Frustrated Customers**: Shoppers are often in a hurry to make decisions, especially when sales promotions are time-sensitive. If they don't receive timely answers to their questions, they become frustrated. For example, if a customer cannot confirm whether a dining set will arrive in time for a holiday dinner, they may choose to shop elsewhere.

2. **Abandoned Shopping Carts**: In e-commerce, speed is critical. If a customer cannot get the information they need promptly, there's a high likelihood they will abandon their shopping cart and leave the site. These lost sales represent missed revenue opportunities that the retailer can't afford to ignore, especially during critical sales periods.

3. **Lost Sales Opportunities**: In addition to cart abandonment, the inability to engage with customers efficiently leads to a direct loss of sales. Some shoppers may not return to the site, having had a negative experience, and instead may go to competitors who provide faster service.

4. **High-Stress Work Environment**: The overwhelming volume of inquiries creates a stressful environment for the customer service team. Agents feel the pressure to respond as quickly as possible, which can lead to burnout, mistakes, and reduced job satisfaction. The constant need to multitask—juggling phone calls, live chats, and email responses—also means that complex customer issues don't get the attention they deserve.

5. **Limited Focus on Complex Issues**: Because agents are inundated with routine questions, they have less time to devote to more complex customer concerns that require thoughtful and personalized responses. This can affect the overall quality of customer service and leave customers feeling undervalued or neglected.

The impact of these problems is clear: the retailer's reputation can suffer, customer loyalty may decline, and the store may miss out on the financial benefits that come with successful sales events. The retailer needs a scalable, efficient solution to handle the surge in customer inquiries while also ensuring a high-quality service experience.

The AI Solution

To tackle these challenges, the online retailer implemented an **AI Customer Service Agent** using advanced technology from **Vapi.ai** for voice-based interactions and **Twilio** for managing SMS communication. This AI-powered system was specifically designed to manage and automate responses to common customer queries, which helped to alleviate the pressure on the human customer service team and improve the overall efficiency of the support operations.

The AI assistant is capable of handling a large volume of inquiries simultaneously, providing immediate, accurate, and helpful responses to customers. By automating routine and frequently asked questions, the AI system allows the human agents to focus on more complex and nuanced customer issues, improving both response times and service quality.

Here's how the system works in detail, and the specific ways it transforms the retailer's customer service experience will be elaborated on in the next sections.

Detailed Workflow

The AI customer service agent is designed to streamline the entire support process for the e-commerce store, from answering routine questions to handling more complex tasks like order updates and returns. Here's a comprehensive breakdown of how the AI assistant manages customer inquiries across different channels and scenarios.

1. 24/7 Customer Support

The AI assistant provides round-the-clock support, meaning customers can get assistance at any time of day, even during off-hours or peak sales periods. This is particularly important for an e-commerce store, where sales opportunities can come from different time zones or late-night shoppers.

- **Voice and SMS Support**:

    - The AI operates seamlessly over both phone and SMS. When a customer calls the support line, the AI answers promptly, using a natural, conversational tone to engage with the caller. It can also respond to text messages with the same level of effectiveness. This dual-channel capability ensures that the AI assistant can meet customers where they are, whether they prefer speaking over the phone or texting.

- **Example of Common Inquiries**:

    - **"What's your return policy?"**: The AI immediately provides a clear explanation of the store's return policy, specifying the conditions for returns, refund timelines, and any applicable restrictions.

    - **"When will my order be delivered?"**: The AI can check shipping details in real time (more on this below) and provide an estimated delivery date, ensuring that customers have all the information they need to track their orders.

- **Natural Language Understanding (NLU)**:

    - The AI assistant is equipped with advanced Natural Language Processing (NLP) capabilities. This allows it to understand and respond to a wide variety of customer queries, even when they are phrased differently or contain multiple questions.

- **Example**: If a customer says, "I need to know if I can return the chair I bought last week, and when will my other order be delivered?" the AI is smart enough to break down the request and provide relevant answers to each part.

- **Human-Like Interaction**: The AI is programmed to use conversational cues and polite language, making the interaction feel more human-like. It can ask follow-up questions, offer additional assistance, and even acknowledge the customer's concerns empathetically. For example, if a customer sounds frustrated or uses negative language, the AI might respond with, "I understand how important this is to you. Let me help you with that right away."

2. Order Status Updates

Keeping customers informed about their orders is a top priority for any e-commerce business. The AI assistant makes this process smooth and efficient.

- **Integration with Order Management System**:
  - The AI is fully integrated with the store's order management system, which means it can access real-time information about a customer's order status, including shipping dates, delivery timelines, and tracking details.
  - This integration allows the AI to provide accurate, up-to-date responses that minimize the need for customers to dig through their emails or contact human agents for updates.

- **Example Conversation**:
  - **Customer**: "Where's my order?"
  - **AI**: "I see that your order was shipped on [date] and is expected to arrive on [date]. Would you like me to send you a tracking link via email or SMS?"

- **Proactive Assistance**: The AI not only provides the information requested but also offers additional help, such as sending a tracking link or explaining how to track the order on the shipping carrier's website

3. Returns and Refunds

Handling returns and refunds is a critical part of customer service, and the AI assistant makes this process simple and efficient for both the customer and the support team.

- **Automated Returns Process**:

  - The AI guides customers through the return process step-by-step, gathering all the necessary details to initiate the return. This includes asking for the order number, the reason for the return, and the condition of the item.

  - **Logging in the CRM**: Once the AI has collected the required information, it logs the return request into the store's Customer Relationship Management (CRM) system. This creates a record that human agents can review and follow up on if necessary. The automation ensures that all details are accurately captured, minimizing errors and speeding up the return process.

- **Self-Service Options**:

  - Customers can initiate returns or request refunds through simple voice commands or SMS. This self-service feature is highly convenient, allowing customers to manage returns at their own pace without waiting for human assistance.

- **Example Interaction**:

    - **Customer**: "I want to return the blender I bought. It's not working properly."
    - **AI**: "I'm sorry to hear that the blender isn't working. May I have your order number to start the return process? Once I have this, I can explain how to proceed and what steps to expect next."

    - **Follow-Up Communication**: If a refund is approved or additional information is needed, the AI can send automated follow-up emails or SMS messages to keep the customer informed.

4. Escalation to Human Support

While the AI assistant is capable of handling a wide range of inquiries, it's designed to recognize when a problem is too complex or requires human intervention. In such cases, the AI ensures a smooth transition to a human agent.

- **Recognizing Complex Issues**:

    - The AI can identify situations where a customer's request goes beyond its programmed capabilities. This might include disputes over billing, complex technical problems, or cases that require a personalized touch.

- **Contextual Transfer**:

    - When escalating a call or message, the AI provides the human agent with a summary of the conversation so far, including the customer's name, the issue they're facing, and any actions already taken. This saves time and prevents the customer from having to repeat themselves, which is a common frustration in traditional support interactions.

- **Example**: "I'm transferring you to one of our support specialists who can assist you further. They have all the details of your request, so you won't have to repeat anything. Please hold for a moment."

- **Prioritizing Urgent Escalations**:

  - If the AI detects that a situation is urgent (e.g., a customer mentions needing immediate assistance for a billing issue or a product defect), it can flag the interaction as high-priority. This ensures that the human support team addresses the issue promptly

Benefits of This Workflow

- **Efficiency**: By automating routine tasks and handling simple inquiries instantly, the AI assistant drastically reduces the workload on the human support team.

- **Customer Satisfaction**: Customers receive quick, accurate, and helpful responses, which improves their overall experience and increases their likelihood of completing purchases and returning to the store in the future.

- **Scalability**: The AI can manage an unlimited number of inquiries simultaneously, making it ideal for handling high volumes of customer interactions during peak sales periods.
- **Reduced Stress for Support Staff**: With the AI managing routine questions and processes, human agents are free to focus on complex, high-value interactions, leading to a more balanced and productive work environment.

This comprehensive, automated approach ensures that the e-commerce store can deliver exceptional customer service even during the busiest times, ultimately driving more sales and boosting customer loyalty.

Use Case 3: AI Cold Caller for a Real Estate Agency

Background

In the highly competitive world of real estate, agents must constantly be on the lookout for new leads to keep their sales pipeline active. This means a substantial portion of their day is often dedicated to **cold calling**—reaching out to potential clients who may or may not be interested in buying or selling a property. This process, while necessary, is incredibly time-consuming and often inefficient.

Consider the typical workday of a real estate agent. They might start the morning with a list of 100 names and numbers, spending hours on the phone just to connect with a handful of potential leads. Most calls result in voicemail, uninterested prospects, or minimal information gathering. Only a small percentage of these conversations turn into actionable opportunities. Moreover, the repetitive nature of cold calling can lead to frustration and fatigue, making it harder for agents to remain motivated and energized throughout the day.

Problem

The core issue is **inefficiency**. Agents are wasting valuable hours on unproductive calls, which has several negative consequences:

1. **Reduced Productivity**: The time spent on cold calling takes away from more valuable tasks, such as showing properties to interested buyers, negotiating contracts, or working with clients who are ready to transact. Essentially, agents are trapped in a cycle of low-value activities, limiting their ability to generate revenue.

2. **Missed Opportunities**: Because agents are busy making calls that often yield no results, they might miss out on opportunities to engage with serious buyers or sellers. For example, if an agent spends three hours cold calling, that's three hours they're not available to meet with a client who wants to view a property.

3. **Burnout and Stress**: Cold calling is one of the least enjoyable parts of being a real estate agent. It requires a high level of persistence and resilience, as rejection rates are high. Over time, the repetitive nature of cold calling can lead to burnout, reduced morale, and even turnover, which impacts the agency's overall performance.

4. **High Operational Costs**: In some agencies, the solution to the cold-calling problem is to hire additional staff, but this increases labor costs and often does not result in a strong return on investment. The resources spent on cold calling could be better allocated if there were a more efficient way to engage potential leads.

The AI Solution

The real estate agency turned to technology to solve this issue, implementing an **AI Cold Caller** powered by **Vapi.ai** and **Twilio**.

This AI assistant is designed to take over the repetitive and time-consuming task of cold calling, allowing real estate agents to focus on what they do best: closing deals and nurturing client relationships.

The AI cold caller is highly sophisticated, capable of engaging leads in a conversational manner, asking pre-qualifying questions, and even scheduling follow-up appointments.

Detailed Workflow of the AI Cold Caller

1. Automated Outbound Calling

The AI cold caller uses advanced conversational AI to make hundreds of calls per day, significantly increasing the volume of leads the agency can reach. Unlike human agents, the AI can call around the clock, optimizing calling hours to reach people when they are most likely to answer.

- **Engaging Introduction**: The AI starts each call with a friendly and engaging introduction, designed to capture the lead's attention. For example:

    - **AI**: "Hello, this is [AI Assistant Name] calling from [Real Estate Agency]. I hope you're having a great day! I'm reaching out to see if you're currently considering buying or selling a home in your area."

- **Authentic and Human-Like Conversation**: The AI is programmed to use a conversational tone, incorporating natural pauses and polite language to make the interaction feel more genuine. It can even handle basic pleasantries or small talk, making the lead feel comfortable.

2. Pre-Qualifying Leads with Targeted Questions

Once the AI has the lead's attention, it asks a series of pre-qualifying questions to determine if the person is a serious prospect. These questions are carefully designed to collect essential information:

- **Current Interest in Buying or Selling**:
  - **AI**: "Are you thinking about buying a new home or perhaps selling your current property sometime soon?"

- **Motivation and Needs**: If the lead expresses interest, the AI dives deeper to understand their motivations and preferences.
  - **Buyer Scenario**: "Great! Do you have a specific budget range or neighbourhood in mind for your next home?"
  - **Seller Scenario**: "Thank you for sharing. Are you hoping to sell quickly, or are you just exploring your options at the moment?"

- **Timeline and Urgency**:
  - **AI**: "When would you ideally like to make this move? Is it within the next few months, or are you planning a bit further out?"

- **Collecting Additional Preferences**: If the lead is a buyer, the AI may ask about their preferred type of home (e.g., single-family, condo) or features they're looking for (e.g., number of bedrooms, backyard space).

3. Capturing and Organizing Lead Information

As the AI interacts with the lead, it captures and organizes all the details in the agency's Customer Relationship Management (CRM) system. This ensures that when human agents follow up, they have all the relevant information at their fingertips.

- **Detailed Lead Profiles**: The AI creates a comprehensive profile for each lead, including:
  - Contact information
  - Answers to the pre-qualifying questions
  - Notes about the lead's motivations, timeline, and specific needs

- **Lead Scoring**: The AI can also assign a lead score based on the information gathered, helping agents prioritize which leads to pursue first.

4. Scheduling Follow-Up Appointments

If the AI identifies a qualified and interested lead, it offers to schedule a follow-up appointment with a human real estate agent. Using Make.com, the AI can:

- **Check Agent Availability**: The AI accesses the agents' calendars to find suitable time slots for property viewings or consultations.

- **Book Appointments**: Once an appropriate time is found, the AI books the appointment and sends confirmation details to both the lead and the agent. This includes a calendar invite with all the necessary information.

- **Automated Reminders**: To reduce the chances of no-shows, the AI sends reminders to the lead via SMS or email, keeping them engaged and informed

5. Handling Unqualified Leads

Not every call will result in a promising lead. When the AI encounters someone who is not interested in buying or selling, it politely ends the conversation and logs this information in the CRM. This helps the agency maintain an up-to-date database of contacts without wasting resources.

- **Graceful Exit**:
  - **AI**: "Thank you for your time today. If your plans change and you're interested in buying or selling in the future, please feel free to reach out. Have a wonderful day!"

6. Smooth Escalation to Human Agents for Complex Cases

For leads that show serious interest or ask questions that the AI cannot handle, the system smoothly escalates the call to a human agent. The AI provides the agent with a summary of the interaction, so the lead does not have to repeat any information.

- **Contextual Transfer**: The AI ensures a seamless handoff by summarizing key details, such as: "This lead is a motivated buyer looking for a property in the $500,000 range and is ready to move within the next three months."

- **Prioritizing High-Value Leads**: The AI flags leads that require immediate attention, ensuring that agents can respond quickly and capitalize on these opportunities.

Benefits and Results

1. Massive Time Savings

- **Automated Cold Calling**: The AI can make hundreds of calls in the time it would take a human agent to make a fraction of that number. This automation frees up agents to focus on high-value tasks, such as meeting with clients and closing deals.

- **Reduced Manual Work**: Agents no longer have to spend hours dialing numbers and facing rejection, which increases overall efficiency.

2. Higher Quality Leads

- **Effective Pre-Qualification**: The AI filters out unqualified leads, ensuring that agents are only working with people who have genuine interest and potential to convert. This improves the overall productivity of the sales team.

- **Lead Prioritization**: By scoring leads based on their responses, the AI helps agents focus on the most promising opportunities first.

3. Increased Productivity and Job Satisfaction

- **Focus on Core Activities**: With the burden of cold calling lifted, agents can dedicate more time to client interactions, property tours, and closing sales. This makes their job more rewarding and less stressful.

- **Reduced Burnout**: The AI handles the repetitive, often discouraging task of cold calling, which can otherwise lead to burnout. Agents can focus on building relationships and delivering value to serious clients.

4. Enhanced Client Experience

- **Efficient and Personalized Service**: Leads who are transferred to human agents experience a smooth and informed transition, as the agent already has a full understanding of their needs and preferences. This makes interactions more efficient and meaningful.
- **Positive First Impressions**: Potential clients are often impressed by the prompt and professional outreach, which reflects well on the agency and builds trust from the very beginning.

Overall Impact on the Real Estate Agency

The implementation of an AI cold caller has revolutionized the way the real estate agency handles lead generation. By automating the cold-calling process, the agency can scale its outreach efforts, qualify more leads, and increase overall efficiency without sacrificing quality.

Agents are more productive, the agency's sales pipeline remains full, and the entire team can focus on what truly matters: building relationships and closing deals. This technology-driven approach sets the agency apart from competitors and positions it for long-term success in a fast-paced market.

Use Case 4: AI Customer Retention Specialist for a Subscription-Based Business

Background

Customer retention is the backbone of subscription-based businesses. Whether it's a meal kit service, a fitness app, or a SaaS (Software as a Service) platform, retaining existing customers is more profitable than acquiring new ones. Loyal subscribers mean predictable revenue, better customer lifetime value, and a strong foundation for growth.

However, many subscription-based businesses struggle with **churn**, the rate at which customers cancel their subscriptions. Churn is expensive and disruptive, often leaving businesses scrambling to acquire new customers just to break even.

Real-world Scenario: A meal kit delivery service notices a troubling trend: nearly 40% of customers cancel after the first month. The reasons vary—some cite dissatisfaction with the menu options, others mention delivery delays, while some simply forget to renew. Each cancellation represents lost revenue, but more importantly, it's a missed opportunity to address the customer's concerns and retain them.

Problem

Managing churn is a resource-intensive process:

1. **High Churn Rates**: Many customers cancel without giving feedback, leaving the business in the dark about how to improve its offerings.

2. **Limited Time and Resources**: The customer service team cannot personally reach out to every at-risk subscriber, especially as the customer base grows. This means opportunities to retain customers are often missed.

3. **Generic Messaging**: Many retention strategies rely on generic email campaigns that lack personalization, failing to address specific customer concerns.

4. **Missed Feedback Opportunities**: Without understanding why customers are leaving, the business cannot make meaningful improvements to its services.

5. **Customer Dissatisfaction**: Engaging with customers after they've decided to leave is often too late, making proactive retention strategies essential.

The AI Solution

To tackle these challenges, the subscription-based business implemented an **AI Customer Retention Specialist** using **Vapi.ai** for voice-based engagement and **Twilio** for SMS and email communication. This AI-driven system automates proactive retention efforts, identifying at-risk customers, engaging them with personalized messages, and offering solutions tailored to their needs. This isn't a one-size-fits-all tool—it's a dynamic, data-driven assistant designed to save customers before they churn.

Detailed Workflow

Here's how the AI Customer Retention Specialist works in practice:

1. Identifying At-Risk Customers

The AI integrates with the business's existing systems, such as its subscription management software, CRM, and analytics platforms. It uses machine learning to analyze customer data and identify patterns that indicate churn risk.

- **Key Indicators of Churn**:
    - **Inactivity**: Customers who haven't logged into their accounts or used the service in a set period.
    - **Negative Feedback**: Customers who've rated the service poorly or submitted complaints.
    - **Cancellation Attempts**: Subscribers who've initiated cancellation but didn't complete the process.
    - **Renewal Hesitation**: Customers nearing the end of a trial period or subscription cycle who haven't renewed.

- **Real-Time Tracking**: The AI continuously monitors customer behavior to flag at-risk subscribers, prioritizing those most likely to churn.

Example: The AI flags Sarah, a subscriber who hasn't ordered a meal kit in three weeks and ignored a recent promotional email.

2. Proactive Engagement with At-Risk Customers

Once at-risk customers are identified, the AI reaches out to them through their preferred communication channel (voice, SMS, or email).

- **Voice Calls with Vapi.ai**:

    - The AI calls the customer, using natural, conversational language to engage them.
    - **Example Interaction**:
        - **AI**: "Hi Sarah, this is Alex from [Meal Kit Service]. I noticed you haven't placed an order in a while. Is there something we can do to improve your experience?"
        - **Customer**: "I didn't like the vegetarian options."
        - **AI**: "Thank you for your feedback! We've recently added more variety to our vegetarian menu, including high-protein options. Would you like to give it another try with a $10 discount on your next order?"

- **SMS and Email with Twilio**:

    - The AI sends personalized messages tailored to the customer's situation.
    - **Example SMS**: "Hi Sarah, we noticed you haven't used your meal kit subscription recently. Try our new vegetarian dishes this week—here's a $10 coupon to make it easier: [Link]."

- **Dynamic Messaging**: The AI adjusts its tone and content based on customer behavior. For example:

    - For a highly engaged customer: "We miss you! Come back and enjoy your favourite meals again."
    - For a less-engaged customer: "Here's a special offer to help you rediscover our service: [Discount Link]."

3. Offering Tailored Retention Strategies

The AI doesn't stop at engagement—it actively works to retain customers by offering solutions that address their concerns:

- **Discounts and Loyalty Rewards**:

    - If cost is a barrier, the AI offers targeted discounts or loyalty perks.
    - **Example**: "We'd hate to see you go. How about 20% off your next three months if you stay with us?"
- **Service Modifications**:

    - If dissatisfaction stems from service issues, the AI provides alternatives.
    - **Example**: "Would you like to pause your subscription instead of canceling? We'll keep your account on hold until you're ready to return."
- **Personalized Recommendations**:

    - The AI suggests features or plans tailored to the customer's preferences.
    - **Example**: "We noticed you enjoy vegetarian dishes. Our new plant-based options might be perfect for you. Would you like to switch your plan?"

4. Collecting Feedback

Even if a customer decides to cancel, the AI gathers valuable feedback to help the business improve.

- **Conversational Feedback Collection**:

    - **AI**: "I'm sorry to hear you're canceling. Could you share what we could have done better?"
    - **Customer**: "The delivery times didn't work for me."
    - **AI**: "Thank you for sharing. We're working on offering more flexible delivery slots. Would you be open to trying us again in the future?"

- **Data Analysis**: The AI compiles feedback into actionable reports, helping the business identify common pain points and prioritize improvements.

5. Seamless Escalation to Human Retention Specialists

For cases requiring a personal touch, the AI smoothly transitions the conversation to a human agent.

- **Contextual Handoff**: The AI provides the agent with a detailed summary of the interaction so far, including the customer's feedback and any offers made.
    - **Example Summary**: "Sarah is considering canceling due to dissatisfaction with vegetarian options. She was offered a discount but hasn't decided yet."
- **High-Priority Notifications**: For urgent cases, the AI flags the account for immediate follow-up by a human team member.

6. Continuous Monitoring and Engagement

After retaining a customer, the AI continues to monitor their activity and sends periodic check-ins to ensure satisfaction.

- **Example Check-In**: "Hi Sarah, how are you enjoying your new vegetarian meals? We'd love your feedback!"

Results and Benefits

1. Reduced Churn Rates:

- The AI engages with at-risk customers before they leave, offering timely solutions that keep them subscribed.

2. Time and Resource Savings:

- By automating retention efforts, the AI frees up human teams to focus on more complex cases, saving both time and money.

3. Enhanced Customer Experience:

- Personalized engagement shows customers that the business values them, improving satisfaction and loyalty.

4. Actionable Insights:

- The AI gathers detailed feedback, helping the business make data-driven improvements to its services.

5. Scalability:

- The AI can manage thousands of interactions simultaneously, making it ideal for businesses with large customer bases.

Real-World Example

Business: A fitness app offering guided workouts and personalized plans.

Problem: Many users cancel after the first month, citing difficulty staying motivated.

AI Solution:

- **Engagement**: The AI reaches out with a motivational call: "Hi [Customer], we noticed you haven't logged a workout recently. Let's get you back on track—here's a free one-week personalized plan!"
- **Retention Strategy**: The AI offers to pause their subscription or provide additional resources like meal plans or coaching tips.

Result: The app retains 25% more customers during its next subscription cycle and identifies key improvements to enhance user engagement.

Chapter 9: Data Security and Compliance

Introduction: Why Data Security and Ethical AI Matter

As a business owner implementing AI voice solutions, protecting your customers' data and ensuring ethical use of AI is critical. Mishandling sensitive information can lead to loss of trust, legal penalties, and even reputational damage. At the same time, ethical AI practices are essential to ensure your technology benefits customers without unintentionally harming or misleading them.

This chapter will guide you step by step through:

1. **How to protect customer data** and comply with regulations like GDPR, CCPA, and PIPEDA.
2. **How to use AI responsibly**, transparently, and ethically.

Let's break it down so you can apply these principles easily, even if you're not a tech expert.

Part 1: Protecting Customer Data

What Is Customer Data?

Customer data includes any information that identifies a person or provides insights about them. For example:

- **Basic information**: Name, phone number, email address.
- **Service-related data**: Call recordings, appointment details, preferences.
- **Sensitive data**: Payment information, medical details (for industries like healthcare).

When using AI tools like Vapi.ai and Twilio, this data passes through and may be stored in various systems. Your responsibility is to keep it secure.

Step-by-Step: How to Secure Customer Data

1. Use Encryption

Encryption ensures that customer data is scrambled and can only be read with a special key.

- **Why It's Important**: If hackers intercept data during a phone call or message, encryption keeps it unreadable.
- **How to Do It**:
    - **For Twilio**: Twilio automatically encrypts voice and messaging data. Ensure this feature is active in your account settings.
    - **For Data Storage**: Use encrypted databases like those offered by cloud services such as AWS or Google Cloud.

Example: If a customer shares their credit card number during a call, encryption ensures it stays secure.

2. Limit Access to Data

Restrict who can see or use customer information in your systems.

- **Why It's Important**: The fewer people with access, the lower the risk of accidental or intentional misuse.
- **How to Do It**:
    - Set **role-based permissions** in your tools (like Vapi.ai or Make.com).
    - Regularly review who has access and remove anyone who no longer needs it.

Example: Only your admin should have access to customer records, while your marketing team might only see anonymized trends.

3. Use Strong Passwords and Two-Factor Authentication (2FA)

Protect accounts with passwords and an extra verification step.

- **Why It's Important**: Even if someone guesses your password, 2FA stops them.
- **How to Do It**:
    - Enable 2FA on tools like Twilio and Make.com.
    - Use password managers like LastPass to create strong passwords.

Example: When logging into Twilio, you'll need both your password and a code sent to your phone.

4. Comply with Data Retention Policies

Only keep customer data as long as you need it.

- **Why It's Important**: Storing unnecessary data increases risk and may violate privacy laws.

- **How to Do It**:
  - Set automatic deletion for old data (e.g., delete inactive customer records after 6 months).
  - Use anonymization for historical data that you need for analytics.

Example: A fitness app deletes a user's data 30 days after they cancel their subscription.

Regulations to Follow

1. GDPR (General Data Protection Regulation)

Applies if you serve customers in the European Union.

- **What You Must Do**:
  - Get customers' explicit consent before collecting their data.
  - Allow customers to access or delete their data upon request.

2. CCPA (California Consumer Privacy Act)

Applies if you serve customers in California.

- **What You Must Do**:
  - Inform customers what data you collect and why.
  - Allow customers to opt out of having their data sold.

3. PIPEDA (Personal Information Protection and Electronic Documents Act)

Applies if you're in Canada.

- **What You Must Do**:
  - Clearly state how data will be used.

- Protect data with encryption and other safeguards.

Quick Tips for Compliance

- Display a privacy notice on your website.
- Regularly review your policies to ensure they meet regulations.
- Use automated tools like Vapi.ai's regulatory features to manage customer data requests.

Part 2: Ensuring Ethical AI Use

What Is Ethical AI?

Ethical AI means using AI in a way that is:

- **Transparent**: Customers know when they're interacting with AI.
- **Fair**: AI treats everyone equally and avoids bias.
- **Accountable**: Your business takes responsibility for how AI behaves.

Principles of Ethical AI

1. Transparency

Let customers know they're interacting with AI, not a human.

Example: Start your calls with, "Hi, I'm an AI assistant from [Your Business Name]. How can I help you today?"

2. Avoid Bias

Bias happens when AI unintentionally favors one group over another.

How to Prevent It:

- Use diverse datasets to train your AI.
- Regularly test your AI responses to ensure fairness.

Example: An AI assistant should recommend properties to buyers without favoring certain neighborhoods unless specified by the customer.

3. Accountability

Ensure a human reviews sensitive decisions or escalations.

Example: For a billing dispute, the AI collects details but passes the case to a manager for final resolution.

Practical Steps for Ethical AI

1. Offer Opt-Out Options

Always let customers speak to a human if they prefer.

Example: "Say 'talk to a representative' at any time to connect with our team."

2. Publish Your AI Policies

Add a page on your website explaining:

- How your AI works.
- How it protects privacy.
- How customers can contact you with concerns.

3. Monitor AI Performance

Regularly review how your AI handles real-world interactions.

Example: Use analytics in Vapi.ai to check if customers' questions are being answered accurately.

Troubleshooting Common Issues

Q: How can I tell if my system is compliant?

- Use Vapi.ai's compliance tools to audit data handling.
- Hire a third-party expert to review your setup annually.

Q: What if a customer complains about privacy?

- Apologize and explain how their data is protected.
- Offer to delete their data if they prefer.

Q: Can AI accidentally make mistakes?

- Yes, which is why regular monitoring and human oversight are important.

Conclusion: Building Trust Through Security and Ethics

Data security and ethical AI are not just responsibilities—they're opportunities to build trust with your customers. By following the practices in this chapter, you'll not only comply with regulations but also create a business that customers feel confident interacting with.

Chapter 10: Future Trends in AI Voice Solutions

Introduction: Preparing for the Future of AI

AI voice solutions are not just a tool for today—they're a gateway to the future of business operations. As technology advances, new trends and features will continue to reshape the way small businesses engage with customers, manage operations, and grow their impact.

In this chapter, we'll cover:

1. **What's next for AI in business**—emerging trends that will revolutionize small businesses.
2. **How to prepare for these changes**—practical tips for staying ahead and continuously improving your AI systems.

Even if you're just getting started, understanding the future can help you plan smarter and set your business up for long-term success.

Part 1: Emerging Trends in AI Voice Solutions

1. Hyper-Personalization: Making Conversations Unique

AI is becoming smarter at tailoring every interaction to the individual customer.

- **What It Means**:
  AI will analyze customer data—such as past purchases, preferences, and previous calls—to make conversations more personalized.

- **Why It Matters**:
  - Customers appreciate feeling recognized and valued.
  - Personalized interactions lead to higher customer satisfaction and loyalty.

Example:
An AI receptionist for a boutique hotel might say: "Welcome back, Sarah! I see you stayed with us last winter. Are you planning another trip for skiing this year?"

Impact for Small Businesses:
Even a small café can use AI to remember customers' favorite drinks or past orders. This small touch can go a long way in building loyalty.

2. Real-Time Multilingual Support: Breaking Language Barriers

Language will no longer be a barrier to great customer service.

- **What It Means**:
  AI voice assistants will be able to recognize and respond in different languages or even translate conversations in real time.

- **Why It Matters**:
  - Small businesses can serve customers in diverse communities or expand to international markets without hiring multilingual staff.

Example:
A real estate agent's AI assistant switches between Mandarin and English during a property inquiry, ensuring seamless communication with clients from different backgrounds.

Impact for Small Businesses:
A small clothing retailer can easily offer customer support in multiple languages, making their online shop accessible to buyers worldwide.

3. Voice Biometrics: The Future of Security

Soon, your voice will be your password.

- **What It Means**:
  AI will use unique voice patterns to authenticate users, making transactions more secure and seamless.

- **Why It Matters**:
  - Protects sensitive customer data.
  - Eliminates the need for PINs, passwords, or other security steps.

Example:
An AI assistant for a fitness center might say:
"Hi John! I've verified your voice. Let's book your personal training session for next week."

Impact for Small Businesses:
Businesses like salons or gyms can use voice biometrics to securely manage appointments and payments without extra effort from customers.

4. Sentiment Analysis: Understanding Customer Emotions

AI is learning to understand how customers feel during a conversation.

- **What It Means**:
  AI voice solutions will analyze tone and mood in real time to identify customer emotions like frustration, happiness, or confusion.

- **Why It Matters**:
  - Helps businesses identify and resolve negative experiences faster.
  - Improves customer satisfaction by responding with empathy.

Example:
A customer calls to complain about a late delivery. The AI assistant detects frustration in their tone and says:
"I'm so sorry for the delay. Let me escalate this to a manager right away."

Impact for Small Businesses:
Even small stores can benefit from showing customers that their concerns are heard and addressed quickly.

5. IoT Integration: Smarter Automation with Connected Devices

AI voice assistants will increasingly integrate with Internet of Things (IoT) devices.

- **What It Means**:
  AI will work alongside devices like inventory sensors, smart locks, or delivery drones to create automated systems.

- **Why It Matters**:
  - Streamlines business operations.
  - Reduces manual tasks and increases efficiency.

Example:
A warehouse's AI assistant can track inventory in real time using connected sensors and notify staff when stock is low.

Impact for Small Businesses:
A small café can use IoT-enabled AI to monitor inventory and reorder supplies automatically when they run low.

6. Affordable and Accessible AI for All Businesses

As technology advances, AI voice solutions are becoming more affordable and user-friendly.

- **What It Means**:
  More small businesses will be able to adopt AI without the need for large budgets or technical expertise.

- **Why It Matters**:
  - Levels the playing field, allowing small businesses to compete with larger companies.

Example:
A family-owned bakery implements an AI receptionist for under $30 a month, enabling them to manage calls efficiently even during peak hours.

Impact for Small Businesses:
Lower costs mean businesses of any size can take advantage of the same tools once reserved for big corporations.

Part 2: Preparing for the Future

Understanding the trends is one thing—getting ready for them is another. Here are actionable steps to prepare your business for the future of AI voice solutions.

1. Stay Updated on AI Trends

AI evolves quickly, and staying informed is key to staying ahead.

- **What You Can Do**:
  - Follow blogs, newsletters, and webinars from platforms like Vapi.ai, Twilio, and Make.com.
  - Join AI communities online to learn from others in your industry.

Example:
Sign up for an "AI in Small Business" newsletter to receive monthly updates on the latest tools and features.

2. Regularly Update Your AI System

AI voice solutions are not "set it and forget it." Regular updates keep them effective.

- **What You Can Do**:
  - Analyze customer interactions quarterly to identify areas for improvement.
  - Update AI scripts to reflect changes in your business, like new services or promotions.

Example:
An AI receptionist for a dental clinic adds responses for new teeth-whitening services after analyzing call logs.

3. Experiment with Emerging Features

New features can set your business apart. Start small and scale up as you see success.

- **What You Can Do**:
    - Test features like multilingual support or sentiment analysis with a specific group of customers.
    - Use pilot programs to gather feedback and refine your approach.

Example:
A spa uses multilingual AI support for its top international clients before rolling it out more widely.

4. Focus on Customer Feedback

Your customers are the best source of insight into how well your AI solutions are working.

- **What You Can Do**:
    - Use surveys or follow-up emails to ask customers about their experience.
    - Adjust workflows and scripts based on their suggestions.

Example:
A clothing retailer's AI assistant adds sizing recommendations after customers request more guidance during calls.

5. Plan for Scalability

As your business grows, your AI solutions should grow with you.

- **What You Can Do**:
    - Choose tools that can handle increasing call volumes and integrate with additional platforms.
    - Plan for future needs, like multilingual support or advanced analytics.

Example:
A subscription box service expands its AI system to handle international inquiries as it grows globally.

Conclusion: Embrace the Future of AI

AI voice solutions are constantly evolving, and the businesses that embrace these changes will be the ones that thrive. By staying informed, experimenting with new features, and focusing on your customers, you can ensure your business is ready for the future.

What's Next?
The journey doesn't stop here! Check out in this book series, *"AI Customer Retention Strategies for Small Businesses,"* to explore how AI can help you build lasting customer relationships.

Thank you for exploring this exciting world of AI voice solutions with us—here's to your success!

Conclusion

Congratulations on Completing the Journey!

You've reached the final chapter of this guide, but your real journey is just beginning. By diving into AI voice solutions, you've unlocked a powerful toolset that has the potential to transform your business—making it more efficient, customer-focused, and future-ready.

Throughout this book, we've explored practical ways to bring AI into your daily operations. Whether you're a small retail shop, a busy medical clinic, or a growing e-commerce store, AI voice solutions can revolutionize how you work and connect with customers.

Let's revisit the incredible possibilities you've uncovered and chart a clear path to your next steps.

Recap: The Key Takeaways from Your AI Playbook

1. AI Voice Solutions Simplify and Scale Your Operations

No longer do you need to spend hours answering calls, following up on inquiries, or managing repetitive tasks. AI voice solutions can handle these with ease, saving you time, money, and effort.

2. You Now Know How to Build Your Own AI Voice System

- With **ChatGPT**, you can craft conversational scripts that reflect your brand's voice and professionalism.

- Using **Vapi.ai**, you can build a customized AI assistant that handles real-world conversations.
- **Make.com** connects all the moving parts, automating workflows behind the scenes to ensure everything runs seamlessly.
- **Twilio** enables your AI to interact through phone calls and SMS, bridging the gap between technology and human interaction.

3. Practical Use Cases for Every Business

We've seen how small businesses can use AI voice assistants to:

- Greet customers and answer common questions with an **AI Receptionist**.
- Boost sales with an **AI Cold Caller** that pre-qualifies leads.
- Deliver exceptional support with an **AI Customer Service Specialist** that's available 24/7.

These are just a few examples of how AI voice solutions can address your business's specific needs.

4. Ethics and Security Are Key

Incorporating AI responsibly means protecting customer data and complying with regulations like GDPR and CCPA. It also means using AI transparently and ethically, earning your customers' trust while delivering outstanding service.

5. The Future is Bright with AI

You've learned about exciting trends like hyper-personalization, voice biometrics, and multilingual support. The AI solutions you implement today can evolve and grow with your business, keeping you ahead of the curve in a competitive market.

Call to Action: Build Your AI Voice Solution Today

You've seen the potential. Now it's time to act. Whether you're excited about automating your calls or curious about testing AI for lead generation, the first step is always the hardest—but it's also the most rewarding.

Here's how to move forward:

1. Start Small

Choose one area of your business to focus on. For example:

- If missed calls are an issue, start by setting up an AI receptionist to handle voicemails and basic inquiries.
- If lead generation takes too much of your time, build an AI cold caller to qualify prospects.

Starting small will allow you to see quick wins while building confidence in your AI system.

2. Use the Tools You've Learned About

- **ChatGPT:** Craft scripts that sound natural, engaging, and professional.
- **Vapi.ai:** Design and deploy your AI voice assistant with features tailored to your business.
- **Make.com:** Automate backend workflows like scheduling, CRM updates, and email notifications.
- **Twilio:** Integrate voice and SMS communication to make your AI assistant feel real and accessible.

Each of these tools has been covered in detail in this book, so you already have the roadmap to implement them.

3. Test, Learn, and Grow

- **Launch Your AI Solution**: Test your system with a small group of customers or staff.
- **Gather Feedback**: Ask for honest input on how the AI performs. Use this to refine scripts, workflows, and responses.
- **Expand Gradually**: Once your first use case is successful, scale up by adding new features or use cases.

4. Stay Curious and Open to Innovation

AI is constantly evolving, and by keeping up with trends, you can stay ahead of the competition. Look out for opportunities to add emerging features like real-time language translation, sentiment analysis, or voice biometrics.

Resources to Empower Your Journey

Essential Tools

- ChatGPT: Generate AI-driven scripts tailored to your business's tone and needs.
- Vapi.ai: Build AI voice assistants that fit seamlessly into your operations.
- Make.com: Automate backend workflows for maximum efficiency.
- Twilio: Manage voice calls and SMS for real-time customer interactions.

Educational Content

- Watch setup tutorials on **YouTube** to follow along step by step.
- Enroll in online courses on platforms like **Coursera** or **Udemy** to deepen your understanding of AI.

- Join online communities like Reddit's **r/artificial** or LinkedIn groups for small business owners using AI.

Your AI-Powered Business: A Vision of What's Possible

Imagine this:

- Every customer call is answered, every inquiry is resolved, and your business runs seamlessly—even while you're focusing on other priorities.
- Your team is free to spend time building relationships, innovating, and growing your business.
- You're ahead of the curve, leveraging cutting-edge AI tools to compete with larger companies and create exceptional customer experiences.

That's the future you can build with AI voice solutions.

Final Thoughts: Your Journey Is Just Beginning

The *AI Voice Solutions for Small Businesses* series is here to guide you every step of the way. With each book, you'll dive deeper into specific applications, gaining the confidence and knowledge to make AI work for your unique business needs.

You've taken a bold first step. Now, keep moving forward. Embrace these tools, experiment with new ideas, and watch as your business transforms into an AI-powered success story.

Here's to your success—and to the future of your business!

What's Next? A Series to Help You Master AI

This book is just one chapter in a larger journey. The *AI Voice Solutions for Small Businesses* series is designed to give you everything you need to implement, refine, and scale AI systems in every corner of your business. Here's what's coming next:

1. "AI Receptionist: Revolutionizing Small Business Call Management"
Discover how to set up a 24/7 virtual receptionist to manage incoming calls, schedule appointments, and answer customer questions with professionalism and accuracy.

2. "AI Customer Retention Specialist: Building Loyalty with Technology"
Learn how to use AI to keep customers engaged, reduce churn, and build lasting relationships through personalized communication and follow-ups.

3. "AI Cold Caller: Automating Lead Generation"
This book will guide you through creating an AI-powered cold caller that pre-qualifies leads, schedules follow-ups, and maximizes your sales team's productivity.

4. "AI Customer Service Specialist: Providing 24/7 Support"
Step into the future of customer service with an AI solution that can handle inquiries, resolve issues, and delight your customers around the clock.

5. "AI Debt Collection Specialist: Transforming Collections with AI"
Learn how to use AI to improve overdue account management, increase recovery rates, and maintain positive customer relationships.

6. "AI Voicemail Replacement Services: Never Miss an Inquiry Again"

Replace your traditional voicemail system with an AI-powered service that transcribes messages, flags urgent inquiries, and ensures no customer is left waiting.

7. "AI Personal Assistant: Boosting Productivity and Simplifying Operations"

Explore how AI can act as a virtual personal assistant, managing tasks, scheduling, reminders, and even providing actionable insights for your business.

Glossary of Terms

AI (Artificial Intelligence): The capability of a machine to imitate intelligent human behavior. In this context, AI enables voice assistants to understand and respond to human language.

API (Application Programming Interface): A set of protocols and tools for building software and applications. APIs are crucial for connecting AI voice solutions with other systems like CRMs or calendar apps.

Automation: The use of technology to perform tasks with minimal human intervention. Discussed in relation to workflow automation with Make.com.

Chatbot: An AI program that conducts conversations with users, typically over the internet or via voice. Often synonymous with AI voice assistants in this guide.

ChatGPT: An AI language model developed by OpenAI, used for generating conversational scripts or prompts for voice assistants.

CRM (Customer Relationship Management): Software that helps businesses manage their interactions with current and potential customers. Integration with AI through tools like Make.com automates customer data management.

Encryption: The process of encoding data to prevent unauthorized access. Essential for protecting customer data in AI voice solutions.

Ethical AI: The practice of using AI in a manner that is transparent, fair, and accountable. This book covers ethical considerations in AI deployment.

Fallback Response: A pre-defined response used by AI when it cannot interpret or respond to a user's input, enhancing the system's robustness.

GDPR (General Data Protection Regulation): European Union regulation on data protection and privacy. Compliance is discussed in the context of AI voice solutions.

Intent Recognition: A component of NLP where the AI determines the user's intent based on their input, crucial for directing conversation flow.

IoT (Internet of Things): The interconnection via the internet of computing devices embedded in everyday objects, enabling them to send and receive data. Mentioned as a future integration opportunity for AI voice solutions.

Machine Learning (ML): An AI technique where systems learn from data, identify patterns, and improve over time without explicit programming. ML helps AI voice assistants learn from interactions.

Make.com: Previously Integromat, a platform for creating and automating workflows. Used here to integrate AI voice assistants with other business systems.

Natural Language Processing (NLP): A field within AI that focuses on the interaction between computers and humans through natural language. Essential for voice assistants to understand and generate responses.

NLP (Natural Language Understanding): A subset of NLP focused specifically on machine reading comprehension, interpreting the intent and context behind human language.

PIPEDA (Personal Information Protection and Electronic Documents Act): Canadian privacy law that businesses must comply with regarding personal information. Covered in the chapter on data security.

Script: A pre-written text or set of instructions for an AI voice assistant to follow during interactions. This book details how to create and customize these for business needs.

Sentiment Analysis: The use of AI to interpret and classify emotions within text or speech, enhancing customer service interactions.

Speech Synthesis: The artificial production of human speech, used by AI voice assistants to communicate audibly with users.

Speech-to-Text: Technology that converts spoken words into written text, a fundamental step in how AI processes voice commands.

Text-to-Speech (TTS): Converts text into spoken language, allowing AI to "speak" to the user.

Twilio: A cloud communications platform for building voice and messaging applications. This book explains its use for telephony features in AI voice solutions.

User Experience (UX): Refers to how users interact with and perceive the AI system, indirectly covered in discussions on customer satisfaction and interaction.

Vapi.ai: A platform for creating AI voice assistants. Detailed here for building and customizing voice solutions for small businesses.

Voice Assistant: An AI software that understands and responds to voice commands, the main focus of this book.

Voice Biometrics: The use of voice characteristics for identification or authentication, highlighted as an upcoming trend in AI voice solutions.

Webhook: A method used for real-time communication between web applications, explained in the context of integrating voice solutions with external services.

Workflow: A sequence of tasks or steps performed to achieve a specific outcome, often automated through tools like Make.com in this book.

Appendices

Appendix A: Quick Reference Guide to Tools

This table provides a one-stop resource for the tools mentioned in this guide.

Tool Name	Purpose	Key Features	Website
ChatGPT	Script creation for AI voice assistants	Natural conversations, customizable tone	chat.openai.com
Vapi.ai	Build and manage voice assistants	Voice recognition, responsive calls	vapi.ai
make.com	Automate workflows and processes	Connects apps and automates tasks	make.com
Twilio	Add telephony and SMS capabilities	Call handling, messaging services	twilio.com

Appendix B: Ready-to-Use Script Templates

Below are pre-built script templates for common use cases to save you time and get started quickly.

1. AI Receptionist for Appointment Scheduling

Goal: Handle incoming calls and book appointments.
Script:

"Hello! Thank you for calling [Your Business Name]. How can I assist you today? I can help schedule appointments or provide information about our services.
[Pause for response]
Great! What day and time works best for you? I'll confirm availability in just a moment."

2. AI Customer Service for FAQ Handling

Goal: Respond to frequent customer inquiries.
Script:

"Hello, and welcome to [Your Business Name]! I'm here to answer your questions.
For example, I can provide details on our pricing, hours, and services. What would you like to know?"

3. AI Cold Caller for Lead Generation

Goal: Generate interest and schedule follow-up calls.
Script:

"Hi, this is [AI Assistant Name] calling on behalf of [Your Business]. We help businesses like yours [mention value proposition: e.g., save time, boost sales].
Would you be available for a quick 10-minute discussion next week to explore how we can help?"

Appendix C: Troubleshooting Common Issues

This table lists the most common problems with tools, their causes, and easy solutions.

Problem	Tool	Cause	Solution
Voice assistant does not respond	Vapi.ai	API key missing or incorrect configuration	1. Verify the API key in Vapi.ai settings. 2. Check internet connectivity.
Calls not connecting	Twilio	Phone number misconfiguration or low balance	1. Confirm phone number setup in Twilio Dashboard. 2. Check account balance.
Workflow automation fails	Make.com	Integration errors or broken connections	1. Reconnect apps in Make.com. 2. Verify trigger and action settings.
Script provides vague responses	ChatGPT	Prompt is unclear or lacks specificity	1. Refine the script prompt with more details. 2. Test using sample inputs.
Delay in call handling	Vapi.ai/ Twilio	Server latency or call routing issues	1. Check for high server load. 2. Contact Vapi.ai or Twilio support for routing optimization.
SMS messages not delivered	Twilio	Invalid phone number format	1. Confirm the phone number format (include country code). 2. Retry sending.

Problem	Tool	Cause	Solution
Automation triggers too slowly	Make.com	Overloaded workflows or scheduling delay	1. Optimize workflows for efficiency. 2. Adjust the trigger schedule.
Voice assistant misinterprets input	Vapi.ai	Poor voice recognition or unclear speech	1. Test using clear speech. 2. Adjust voice model settings in Vapi.ai.
API usage exceeds limits	ChatGPT/Twilio	Exceeded free/paid API quotas	1. Upgrade to a higher API usage plan. 2. Monitor API call consumption.
Conversations stop mid-call	Vapi.ai/Twilio	Session timeout or network interruption	1. Increase session duration settings. 2. Check for stable internet connection.
Incorrect appointment scheduling	Make.com	Integration issues with calendars	1. Verify calendar connections. 2. Test appointment workflows manually.
Assistant cannot answer queries	ChatGPT	Missing or outdated training data	1. Update prompts with business-relevant information. 2. Add FAQ details to scripts.
Audio quality is poor	Vapi.ai	Low-quality microphone or connection	1. Use a high-quality microphone setup. 2. Ensure a stable internet connection.
SMS or voice notifications delayed	Twilio	Network congestion or routing problems	1. Retry sending the notifications. 2. Contact Twilio support for routing analysis.
Assistant repeats answers	ChatGPT/Vapi.ai	Looping in script logic	1. Review and simplify conversation logic. 2. Test for redundant prompts.

Appendix D: Cost Estimation Worksheet

Use this simple worksheet to estimate your costs for implementing AI voice solutions.

Monthly Cost Estimation

Tool/Service	Monthly Cost	Setup Fees	Notes
ChatGPT API	$_____	$_____	Usage depends on number of queries.
Vapi.ai Voice Assistant	$_____	$_____	Based on active call volume.
make.com Automation Platform	$_____	$_____	Pricing depends on workflows.
Twilio (Voice/SMS)	$_____	$_____	Cost per call or SMS sent.

Appendix E: Glossary of Key Terms

This glossary explains the key terms used throughout the book.

1. **AI Voice Assistant**: Software powered by artificial intelligence that can interact with humans using voice commands.
2. **Natural Language Processing (NLP)**: Technology that helps machines understand and respond to human speech naturally.
3. **Machine Learning (ML)**: AI technology that enables systems to learn and improve over time by analyzing data.
4. **API (Application Programming Interface)**: A connection that allows different software programs to work together.
5. **Workflow Automation**: Using software to streamline repetitive tasks, reducing manual effort.

Appendix F: Checklist for Launching AI Voice Solutions

Follow this checklist to ensure your AI voice solutions are successfully implemented and optimized.

1. Planning and Setup

- Decide the primary tasks for your AI voice assistant (e.g., scheduling, answering FAQs, outbound calls).
- Choose tools: ChatGPT, Vapi.ai, Make.com, Twilio.
- Register for required accounts and obtain API keys.

2. Script Development

- Write initial scripts using templates provided (Appendix B).
- Test conversational flow to ensure clarity and effectiveness.

3. Tool Integration

- Set up Vapi.ai for voice recognition.
- Automate workflows using Make.com.
- Configure telephony and SMS through Twilio.

4. Testing

- Test end-to-end processes with mock calls or workflows.
- Address errors using the Troubleshooting Guide (Appendix C).

5. Optimization

- Gather feedback from customers or team members.
- Improve scripts and workflows based on real-world performance.
- Monitor costs and adjust API usage as needed.

Appendix G: Real-World Case Study Summaries

Here's a quick summary of the use cases mentioned in Chapter 8.

1. **Medical Clinic (AI Receptionist)**

   - **Challenge:** Overwhelmed staff and missed calls.
   - **Solution:** AI assistant scheduled appointments and handled patient inquiries.
   - **Results:** 40 hours saved monthly, 25% fewer missed appointments.

2. **E-commerce Store (AI Customer Service)**

   - **Challenge:** Handling high inquiry volumes during peak seasons.
   - **Solution:** AI assistant automated FAQ responses and order updates.
   - **Results:** Faster response times and improved customer satisfaction.

3. **Real Estate Agency (AI Cold Caller)**

   - **Challenge:** Low lead conversion rates.
   - **Solution:** AI cold caller generated leads and scheduled follow-up calls.
   - **Results:** 30% increase in client engagement in three months.

4. **Subscription Business (AI Retention Specialist)**

   - **Challenge:** High churn rate.
   - **Solution:** AI assistant identified at-risk customers and implemented retention strategies.
   - **Results:** 15% improvement in customer retention rates.

www.ingramcontent.com/pod-product-compliance
Lightning Source LLC
Chambersburg PA
CBHW071031240526
45469CB00006BD/2166